Making Children's Furniture and Play Structures

Making Children's Furniture and Play Structures

By Bruce Palmer

Illustrations by Judith Lane

WP Workman Publishing Company, New York

Designed by Paul Hanson
Illustrations by Judith Lane

Typeset by Vermont Photo-Tape Services

Printed by the George Banta Company

ISBN: Hardbound 0-911104-24-0
Softbound 0-911104-25-9

Workman Publishing Company
231 East 51st Street
New York, New York 10022

First printing October, 1974

For my assistants: "Mash" and Maria,
John, Katie and David, Elizabeth,
Diane, Yvonne and Catherine, Anne,
Allison and Ames, Chris, Brook,
Megan and Andrew.

Acknowledgements

The basic geometric forms that shape and enclose the spaces around us were conceived by the Grand Original Designer and displayed in the first snowflake. Our building and decorating materials are processed from natural, organic substances or manufactured by synthesizing new by-products and compounds. We were given the right angle, the cube and parallel lines; and trees for lumber, ore for nails. As a race, we have been building shapes and shelters for eons, constantly varying and expanding the potentials of these prehistoric gifts. From some unknown time, in our leisure, we have made shapes, structures and shelters to protect and amuse our young, for they, too, are born with the itch to make and unmake. Our work has become their play-stuff.

In recent decades, modern design and manufacturing technology, plus the media explosion, has vastly expanded our abilities to build swiftly, safely and at low-cost. Buckminster Fuller's concepts and coupling-systems now spawn domes and zomes in mushroom profusion all over the globe. Exposition buildings, schools, theaters and homes grow everywhere from the basic triangle. Wood-resins and petroleum-based plastics enable us to shape space and cover it with new skins for protection and privacy.

Costs have mounted, too, and collaborations and confederacies of young architect-designers have found new ways to work new materials and ancient shapes, publishing their concepts and creations, aptly titled, like NOMADIC FURNITURE. Perhaps the major disseminator of ideas for low-cost constructions for furniture and housing has been the marvelous WHOLE EARTH CATALOG, its recent supplements and DOME BOOKS. The Alaskan sourdough's stove from a 50-gallon oil drum has evolved through a dozen minds in a dozen years to become fibre-barrel furniture and children's beds or a sun-warmth absorbing wall that can heat a desert home. Cardboard, originally solid, later corrugated, manufactured by the millions of tons ... and wasted ... has now become a common, cheap building material, recycling whole forests into inexpensive, study furniture of all kinds.

We owe a debt, also, to the men and women of the *Bauhaus* movement of the late 1920's, who showed us all again the beauty and strength of basic materials and shapes. Not every good idea and useful skill is native to America. A number of Scandinavians retaught us the natural elegance of wood-grain, so we could know again how to have more from less. We hand on this whole tradition to our young through construction classes in our schools and by making our own homes and apartments into weekend workshops.

On a final personal note, my thanks to Steve Caney for his suggestions and advice.

Bruce Palmer, September, 1974

Contents

Introduction

The apartments and houses we share with children are built, sized and decorated for us, not for them. On rainy days, they play in the living room or underfoot because there is no place else for them to be. In fair weather, city parks are too few, too far away and too crowded. Suburban yards are often neither large nor private, rather an area that must be shared with flower gardens and a power mower. Indoors or out, kids need play spaces that are theirs alone and furniture and equipment designed to meet their needs.

Most of the stuff designed for indoor play comes in three styles only: heavy, with wheels that crash into the coffee table and chip paint off the woodwork; flimsy, with 657 small pieces that get lost or give the vacuum cleaner a strangulated hernia; and electric-powered, requiring four type D batteries (not included).

Most play equipment for outdoor use appears to be poorly designed. Bolts will not fit through holes; three crucial pieces are missing. The apparatus weighs as much as a small truck, yet one energetic and unlucky toddler can bring the whole rig crashing down around his ears. You spend all Saturday morning putting the monster up, the afternoon extending your liability insurance coverage, all day Sunday mixing and pouring concrete footings—"just to be really safe." Within two days, the kids are bored stiff with it. The contraption stands in the wind and the rain, unused and rusting slowly into an eyesore.

As one parent to another, I have wasted too much time and money assembling, repairing and throwing out expensive toys and play equipment. Although I live in the country, I, too, have a storage problem: our farmhouse was built in 1789, before the closet really got itself invented. My skill with simple tools is very likely no better than yours, and my patience is exhausted as quickly as my pocketbook. I am incapable of designing anything that I cannot construct.

Most of us do not provide our children—once they are out of the crib—with furniture designed and constructed for them. After infancy, it's flea-market bargains or a gathering of nondescript pieces abandoned by Aunt Martha when she moved to Florida. Often our kids share a room, further lessening what little privacy they have. Soon after the "open classroom" was declared to be an excellent educational environment, alert elementary school teachers began designing and building "quiet spaces" and "study areas" that closed *out* all the open space and provided some measure of privacy, scaled to the size and needs of children.

Careful attention to these conditions has been given to each of the projects found in the pages that follow. Nearly all the designs for play spaces, equipment, and furniture can be executed in light-weight, durable materials that fold flat for easy storage. Many projects are tab-and-slot-together designs that set up rapidly and can be used for multi-purposes. Treated and painted according to directions, many are both indoor and outdoor projects, resistant to hard play, fire and bad weather. All are simple and inexpensive to make. The shapes are, in general, simple geometric forms, and a good number can be created in different sizes according to the age of the child and storage space available. Since the materials are low-cost, a damaged piece can be replaced and a popular project rebuilt.

Some manufacturers of play equipment boast that their equipment is so rigid and stable that when in use, only children move. But this is contrary to the nature and needs of children. Materials should move too. If a given project or play space is easily assembled, that means it can be as easily taken apart, manipulated, reworked or re-invented—played with, in short.

Play is the work that children do. Play is not amusement or "killing time." It is learning. It is problem-solving. Therefore, kids should be involved in the making process right from the start: first the selection of the project, then on through cutting, shaping, reinforcing, painting, and assembling. After that, kids determine the remaking process. Adults and parents should permit variations of form and encourage development of children's huge energies and imaginations. When a child takes something apart, he is not necessarily wrecking it. He is, instead, discovering what makes it "go;" how to rebuild it, how to make it—in his own mind—better.

Active children are great risk-takers and require supervision. A word or two about safety then. Even a feather can be a dangerous weapon. A child, unwatched and unguided, can fall off anything. Any object that stands can be made to tip over. Children always use play spaces and equipment in ways unthought of by the designer and builder. Any space or piece of equipment worth playing in or with is certain to attract more children than expected. Cardboard bends and wood splinters. Nothing and no one is totally safe. Risk is involved. Don't eliminate risk, cushion the shocks. Provide real cushions with play spaces and equipment. Thick sheets of rubber foam in and around these projects prevent anxious over-attentiveness.

The projects here have been engineered for hard use, the assumption being that each is, to some degree, disposable or impermanent. Children can exhaust the potentials of a given space or piece of equipment quite rapidly. Supervision, then, might well mean "substitution" at times. Adults can help to change a piece or provide another, getting the kids to knock down and store what no longer interests them. A too-familiar object enchants anew, if it disappears and then comes back again. If you have worked with the children to make these projects their play, play with them to help make the projects work. Your care is the softest cushion for your children's experiences.

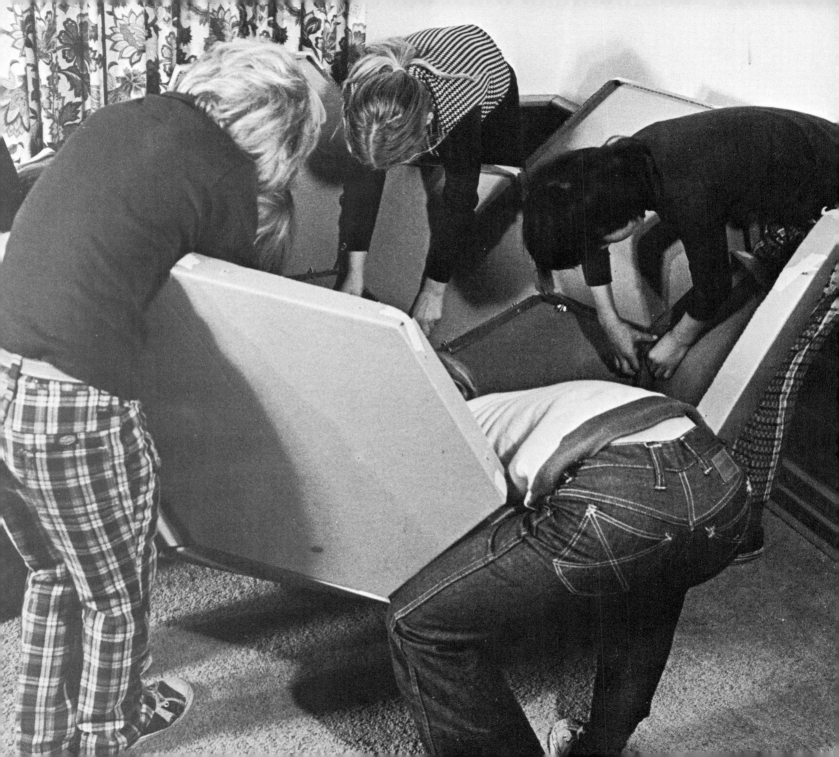

Basic tools and materials

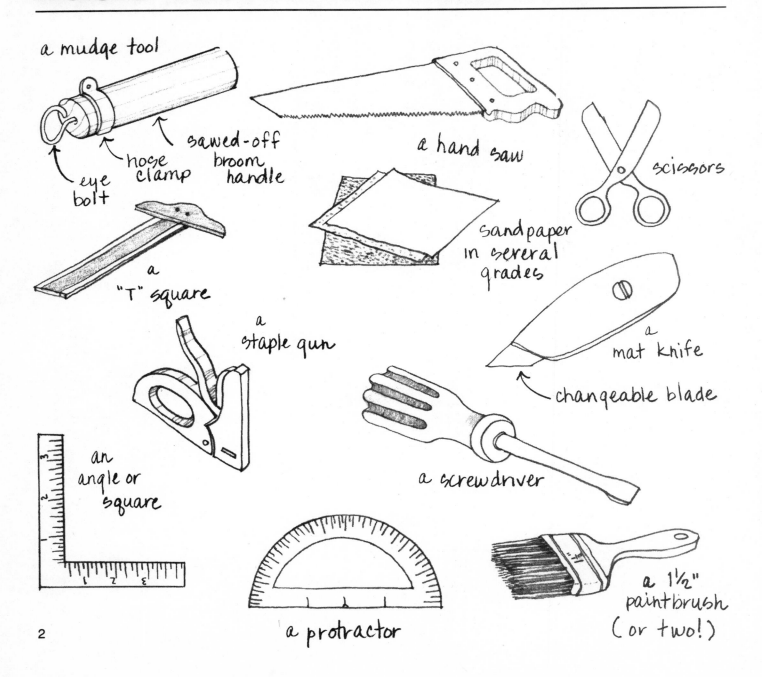

a mudge tool

eye bolt

hose clamp

sawed-off broom handle

a hand saw

scissors

sandpaper in several grades

a "T" square

a staple gun

a mat knife

changeable blade

an angle or square

a screwdriver

a protractor

a 1½" paintbrush (or two!)

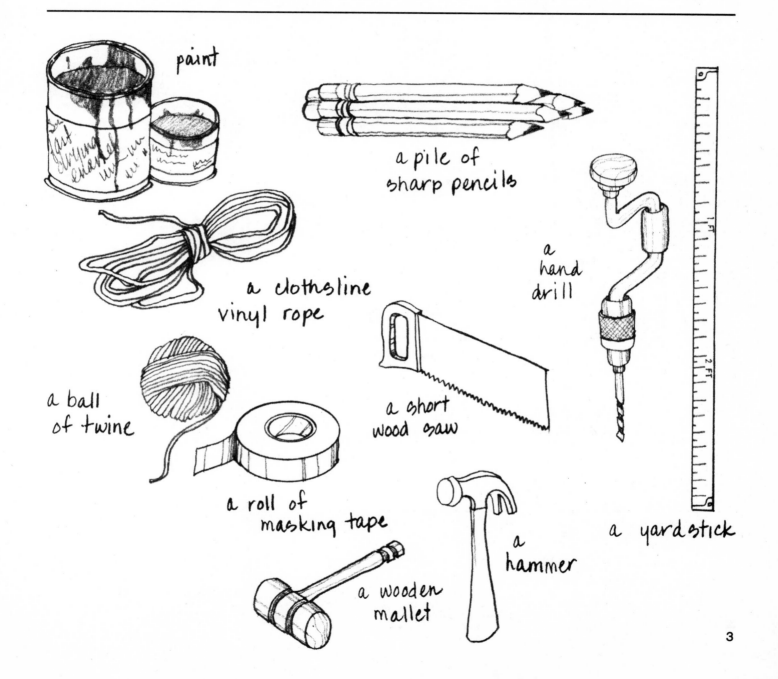

paint

a pile of
sharp pencils

a clothsline
vinyl rope

a hand
drill

a ball
of twine

a short
wood saw

a roll of
masking tape

a wooden
mallet

a
hammer

a yardstick

3

Corrugated cardboard

Most corrugated cardboard can be obtained free. Pieces are discarded everyday by supermarkets, local groceries, and hardware or appliance stores. It is an ideal material to work with—strong and crush-resistant but easily managed by children. You don't have to be a carpenter or true craftsman to use it either. The material forgives marginal error. Basic work can be done with simple hand tools, and small builders don't need adult muscles. Cardboard can be cut, sawed, taped, stapled, doweled, glued, and laced. It can also be fireproofed, waterproofed, painted, or sprayed.

There are a few different types of corrugated. The most common is a sandwich of two thin facings glued to a fluted sheet of the same material. This three-piece combination makes up a single wall, hence the trade name single-wall corrugated.

Double-wall corrugated is a five-layer combination frequently used for industrial containers and to package heavy household appliances.

Triple-wall corrugated, ½" and sometimes 9/16" thick, is a real club sandwich. Immensely strong for its weight (about one-third that of comparably sized plywood), it is considerably less expensive than any solid, compound, or laminated wood product. Some suppliers call this ultimate corrugated "1100-pound," which is its test weight.

What gives corrugated sheets their great strength is the fluting, which absorbs impact and distributes stress. In double- and triple-wall corrugated the fluting often is not the same size, which means that a hill on one sheet may be a valley on the other.

single wall

double wall

triple wall

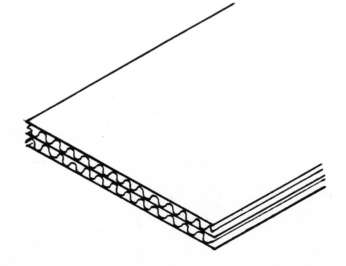

Fiberboard and hardboard

One of the principles of low-cost construction is to reuse some of the widely available materials employed by industry and commerce in new and different ways. The barrels and tubs in which chemicals, detergents, and other dry goods are shipped—also mailing tubes—are great shapes to work with, and all have been put to use in many of the play spaces and furniture designs in this book. They are made of fiberboard or hardboard, both of which can be cut with a mat knife or fine-bladed saw and finished off with fine sandpaper. Fiberboard is made from recycled paper mixed with other materials. Hardboard, a compound of lumber wastes and by-products, recycled paper, and rags, is the tougher and springier of the two.

If you can't find any discarded containers (see Scavenger's Rule 1), you can buy them used or new. Check in the classified phone directory under *"Containers," "Fiberboard Products," "Boxes, Fiber and Corrugated," "Barrels and Drums,"* and *"Tubing."* Always find out what used barrels contained and clean them out carefully. For cleaning, use a brush and dust-pan, then a damp rag or sponge.

Fiberboard tubes and barrels come in standard diameters of 10″, 13″, 18″, 24″, and 36″. Much like the "two-by-four," they run a little smaller than their given dimensions. Firms carry standard lengths, though this usually means the lengths most requested by their steady customers.

Scavenger's rule 1.   Before you buy something, find out whether it's available free. Never pay for something when you can get it for nothing. Try everybody. Begin with an appliance store or warehouse, then visit furniture stores, rug marts, and local industries for fiberboard tubes and used barrels. Check streets for discards. Don't forget liquor stores and drug stores. All these places discard standard-size shipping cartons and boxes every day, so go regularly.

Scavenger's rule 2.   Never refuse anything big. Take a refrigerator carton with a bad rip or crushed corner. Cannibalize other materials and use this first big container to nest all other finds. This way you will have a single object to get back home.

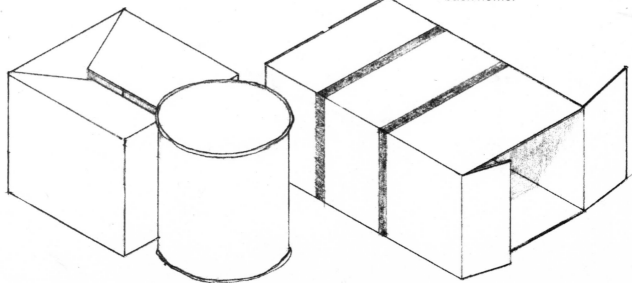

Cutting corrugated materials

Start with a handy-sized piece of single-wall board, your carpenter's square, and your mat knife. Measure a dozen or so inch-width strips across the corrugation, marking them with a sharpened pencil. Place the cardboard on a level cutting surface—a bread board, plywood sheet, or smooth plank will do. Bring the steel edge of the carpenter's square up so it touches the pencil line. Place the knife blade against the edge of the square. Press down firmly on the square, then press and draw the blade down, keeping it snug against the steel edge of the square. Slice off a dozen strips, then check for evenness. You will

notice some variation if you allowed the knife blade to wander away from the guiding edge or let the square itself skid on the board. Don't try to cut with the tip of the blade. Hold the knife at a low angle and keep the angle constant. Practice for perfection. In a short time, you will be able to slice single-wall board with a sure motion.

Double-wall board should be slit twice, *from the same side.* Let the blade do the work or you risk tearing the board.

Since triple-wall board is over a half-inch thick, you cannot cut through it very easily with a knife. Greater accuracy is achieved if you lay out all your measurements on *both* sides before you begin to cut. Draw the blade firmly, but don't put all your weight on the tool. Using a sharp knife you can cut half way through without great effort. Then turn the material over and cut along the lines you drew on the back. If you have been reasonably careful in measuring, the board will be cut precisely as you require it. Double measuring is a must when making slots, since you need a neat, accurate fit.

Curved lines are more easily cut with scissors. Rough out first, then trim. Single- and double-wall board can be sandpapered, using a sheet of fine grit or emery paper. If you try to use your knife, you will find that you either punch and poke along the curved line or slice on an angle that may ruin your work.

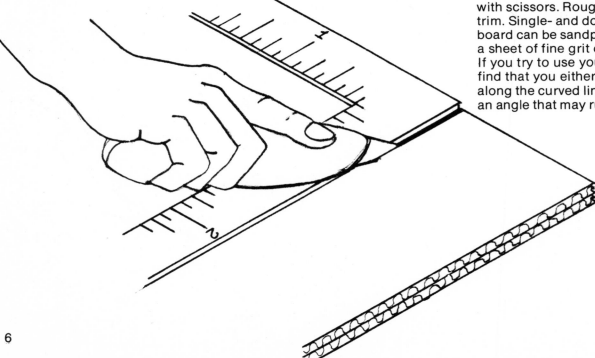

Scoring corrugated

Score corrugated so it will bend without breaking. Be certain that you score on the side you will crease.

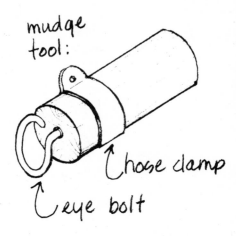

mudge tool:

hose clamp

eye bolt

For easy scoring make yourself a "mudge-tool." I first came across one of these in 1949 in the hands of a Bostoner named Ernie Mudge who concocted odd-shaped boxes for shipping hardware parts. The eyebolt is the scoring edge. It rides flat against your straightedge and with firm pressure makes every score uniform and accurate. Screw it into a length of broom handle or other scrap wood. The hose clamp is for strength only; it keeps the eyebolt from exerting too much pressure on the wood.

You will be scoring single-wall board only. Double- and triple-wall are too thick to fold accurately. Always use a straightedge with your mudge-tool.

Important construction detail: remember that a right-angle score and bend will "shrink" the sheet you are working on by one-half the thickness of the board.

A 180° score and bend (for those occasions when you want to give single-wall extra strength and rigidity) will shrink the sheet by two *thicknesses* (one-half thickness for each score, of course, but one thickness to allow for the foldover to lie flat.)

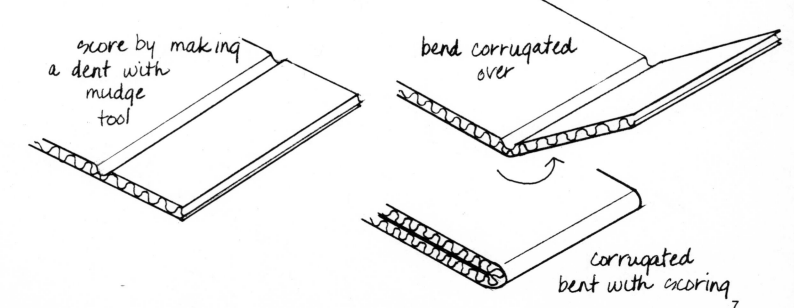

score by making a dent with mudge tool

bend corrugated over

corrugated bent with scoring

Corners and reliefs

All scored and bent single-wall cardboard, when folded into flaps for fastening, will also shrink by one board thickness. Even in small projects this loss can be critical, and you must allow for it. Generally, shrinkage will occur at corners. Therefore, even simple corners need a *relief cut* to prevent the material from humping or bunching. In the diagram below, material has been cut and scored. For relief, pass a rat-tail file between flaps A and B a few times. A tiny effort, but a professional trick that will ensure crisp corners and precise fit.

The next diagram illustrates a corner with relief and *offset*. The material has been cut, then the relief cut made. Position a piece of scrap vertically along score line

and mark its thickness with a pencil. Now score offset line, and you have allowed for a one-thickness shrink. Flap A will tuck neatly under flap B.

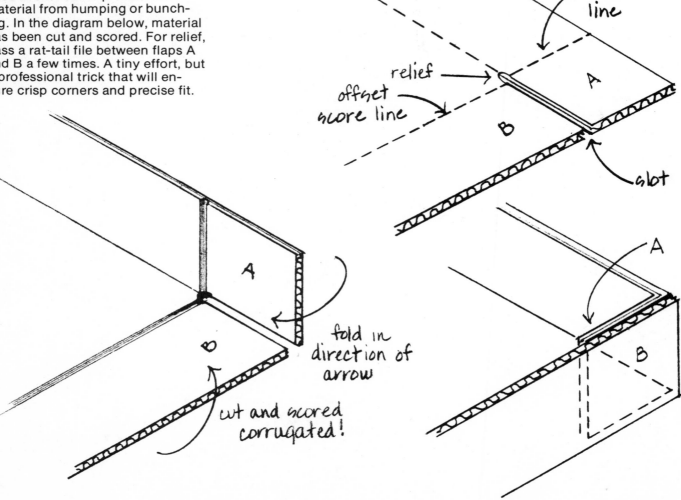

score line

relief

offset score line

slot

A

B

fold in direction of arrow

cut and scored corrugated!

A

B

8

Templates or patterns

Whatever furniture you're making, templates, or patterns, are recommended. For more complex play spaces, especially the dome designs, templates are a must. A template is not material lost, since it can be incorporated into the final assembly to become part of the project.

Measure the shape you need carefully, and cut out the first piece from your corrugated as neatly as you can. Use this piece as a template by placing it on another sheet and drawing around it. Turn the new sheet over, place the template in the same position on the back, draw around it, and you are ready to cut. There will be a very slight gain, since your lines will lie outside the dimensions of the template. Fortunately, however, corrugated is very forgiving stuff. A sixteenth—even an eighth—of an inch one way or the other makes no difference really. And remember, you are only cutting cardboard.

It is likely that you will make some mistakes at first, either by mismeasuring or cutting imperfectly. Don't despair. Even if the mistake is a good-sized one, you can salvage most of the material through canny figuring on later projects. And small scraps will come in handy for struts and braces. The very oddness of their shape or size may well provoke a creative brainstorm for a new project of your own design.

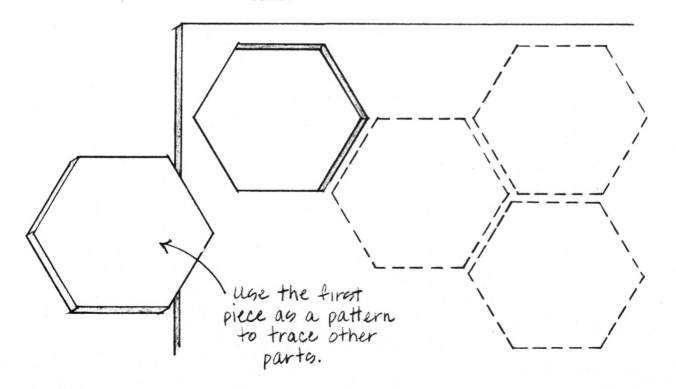

use the first piece as a pattern to trace other parts.

9

Fastening corrugated

Always use contact cement. This is available at paint and hardware stores in both spray cans (handy but expensive) and pint and quart containers. *Never use a brush with contact cement.* Daub or smear glue on corrugated pieces with a tongue depressor and discard stick after use. Avoid all white glues. These are too weak. Model maker's cement and epoxy compounds are also impractical. They are strong but too expensive.

Conventional bolts, washers, and wing-nuts will hold thin corrugated panels together fairly well. Washers distribute the stress to some degree, and the corrugated itself is very strong. (The Workshop for Learning Things markets wooden nuts and bolts that are easy for small fingers to assemble. See Appendix.) Triple-wall corrugated is really too thick for hardware fasteners.

The important thing to remember if you buy or rent a staple gun is to get one that will throw long, wide staples. Use a gun with double- or triple-wall corrugated only, for then the sharp tips of the staples will be buried safely. Staples are particularly good for use on flaps and corners.

As for tape, 3-M masking tape in 1 and 1½″ widths is the best type for our uses. All masking tapes are silicon-coated, so they have good grab and won't creep. However, they need primer before painting. Mover's tape (slick-finished plastic) has excellent grab, too, but it will split and cannot be painted at all. Filament tapes are useful for hinges and have extra strength. These are available at hardware stores in various colors and widths. Such tapes have good grab, no creep, and will not rip. Air-conditioning duct tape in 3″ widths is excellent for play spaces. Duct tape comes in aluminum color only, but it is immensely strong and also waterproof.

Never use scotch-type tapes. And remember, even if you are making a corrugated structure for indoor use only, it is wise to tape all raw edges. Use masking tape; cut short pieces, overlap, and press smooth to prevent bubbling. Do not unroll long strips, or you will find yourself wrestling with sticky snakes!

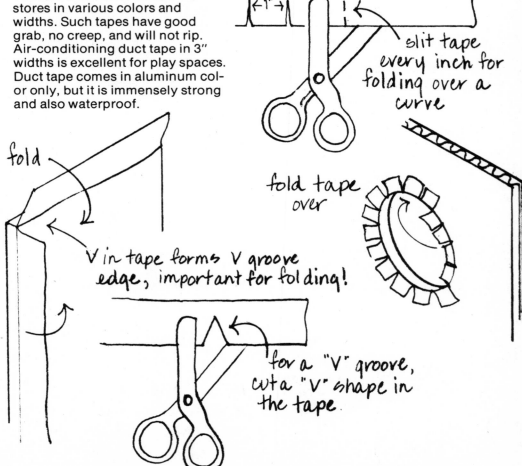

slit tape every inch for folding over a curve

fold tape over

fold

V in tape forms V groove edge, important for folding!

for a "V" groove, cut a "V" shape in the tape.

Sealing, painting, fireproofing

Anything that will be used outdoors must be sealed as well as taped, or it will absorb dirt and moisture (and ants, as I have discovered). Oil-base wall sealer or a lacquer-base automobile primer works best, but both are fairly expensive. Auto paint comes in a variety of unusual colors and gives a marvelous finish. All paint stores carry several brands of waterproof paint. Use one for a base coat and acrylic enamel for finishing.

There is no way to make paper products like corrugated board completely fireproof. Thus if furniture is to be used indoors, you may very well decide to skip this step. However, you *must not* omit fireproofing if the furniture and play spaces you build are intended for use in any kind of school. Fire laws in all states and municipalities are firm on this, and schools are subject to periodic inspections. Moreover, paper products in the classroom are particularly frowned upon. Therefore, if the classroom is the place where your constructions will be used and stored, buy or make yourself some flameproofing and fire-resistant paint and treat *each part* of each piece.

Paper products not only burn, they glow, releasing smoke and gases. The following formula, suggested by the National Bureau of Standards, contains enough ammonium phosphate to inhibit afterglow and to flameproof: diammonium phosphate, 10 oz.; borax, 14 oz.; boric acid, 6 oz.; water, 7 qts. This may yield more fireproofer than you are likely to need. To reduce total volume, simply reduce ingredients proportionately.

Sad to say, all corrugated materials will warp slightly, even triple-wall. If you paint one side only, there will be considerable warp, so it is best to paint both front and back. On the other hand, tubes and barrels of recycled paper or fiberboard normally finish without distortion. Prime coat them first, then add color. As recommended, fireproof if the construction will be used in a school.

A wallpaper and paint store near you probably carries blackboard paint—generally it is green in color. Two coats convert corrugated to wipe-off scribble areas that will take a lot of hard play. The best type of paint to use for decoration as well as protection is acrylic enamel, which is ideal for children's furniture and play spaces made of triple-wall corrugated. Acrylic is odorless and fast-drying, and it usually covers with a single coat, leaving a splendid, soft, semigloss finish that is stain-resistant and weatherproof. It also bonds quite well to masking tapes. If you want to get away from the primary colors so typical of the nursery and kindergarten, have your local paint store custom-mix decorator colors.

Incidentally, as you scavenge through liquor stores, drugstores, and appliance centers, you will come across single- or double-wall corrugated cartons that have been treated with wax. These are fine to work with in slot-together structures, *but they cannot be painted or glued.* So unless you want to spend plenty of money, do not attempt to buy wax-coated (or "calendared") corrugated materials.

A practice project

If you are like me, you have probably flipped to the design that struck you first, and only now are reading the Introduction. Why not begin at the beginning, however, with a practice project that you can build in about an hour?

One of the first things to learn is how to make X-braces. Big shipping containers tend to be weak once their contents are removed, and some are strapped to pieces of wood for fork-lift handling. By contrast, empty liquor cartons are quite strong. A glance at the inside of one should reveal to you the secret of its strength: vertical lining panels, or X-braces. You can very easily make any basic box into a stool, a base, or a support unit for a table by adding scrap corrugated that has been cut into these vertical liners.

First figure out how high off the floor your piece will stand. Then obtain enough corrugated to match your biggest dimension. Now make slots in your corrugated panels. (see p. 18). Each slot must be one-half the height of the panel. For example, if you make two identical pieces that will stand 36″ high, they should be slotted 18″. As they cross they form two sides of an equilateral triangle. Measure from the crossing points to the edges of panel, and you will know how to size your wrapper. Lay wrapper out with ruler and marking pencil, cut, and score it (see page 7) with a mudge-tool. If your first efforts don't succeed, keep practicing.

24″

12″

slot equals one half total panel height

24″

21″

score line on wrapper

combine two panels to form an "X"

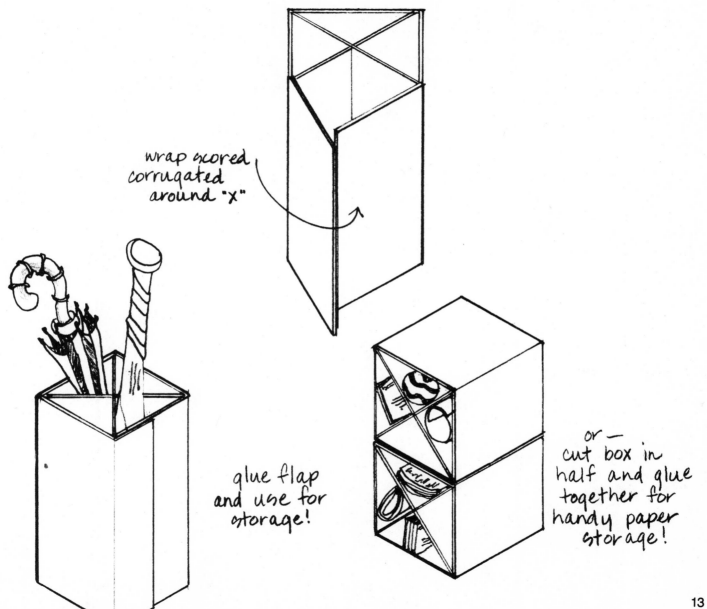

wrap scored corrugated around "x"

glue flap and use for storage!

or —
cut box in half and glue together for handy paper storage!

13

Stools and chairs

Liquor carton stool

Materials

liquor carton (do not remove divider inserts)

masking tape

sand (2 lbs. or more)

acrylic enamel and brush

2" foam cushion (optional)

Weight each carton with a couple of pounds of sand. Cram newspaper balls between dividers. Tape cover down and decorate the whole stool with several coats of acrylic enamel.

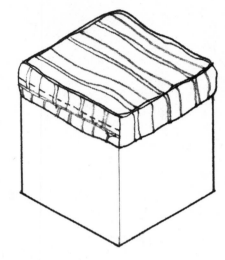

use a liquor carton with dividers intact and add:

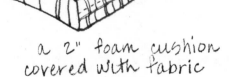

a 2" foam cushion covered with fabric

use newspaper balls for filler and some sand for ballast

16

Barrel stool

Materials

fiberboard barrel, 24″ diameter or bigger

¾″ circular plywood insert

twelve 1″ brass round-head screws

2″ foam cushion (optional)

sand

electric saber saw

screwdriver

Salvage a damaged fiberboard barrel and weight it with sand. Make a plywood insert to fit and fasten to the barrel with screws placed evenly around the circumference of the barrel. Add foam cushion for a strong and comfortable stool; remove the cushion and you can use barrel as an end table.

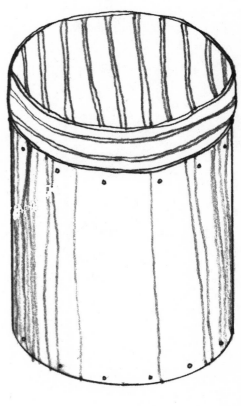

screws hold plywood insert

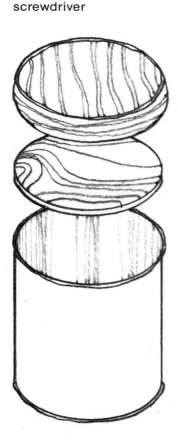

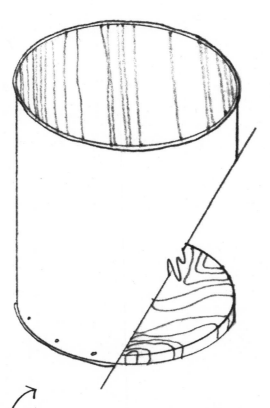

turn barrel over insert and drill holes

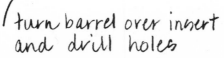

Double- or triple-wall stool

Materials

six pieces double-wall corrugated, 18" square, *or* one sheet triple-wall corrugated, 48" × 72"

masking tape

acrylic enamel and brush

contact cement

2" foam cushion (optional)

ruler or other straightedge

mat knife

marking pen or pencil

This is an easy, quick, and cheap project, ideal for beginners or children. Four slotted sides are assembled and glued on top and bottom. There are three steps to making a slot: (1) mark around scrap piece for length and thickness; (2) cut with mat knife; and (3) pull scrap free and trim.

For a permanent stool, use contact cement to glue the top and bottom down. If you want a storage stool (3 cu. ft. capacity), make a removable insert-panel top. (Insert panel fits snugly inside stool and holds top in place.) To make a knock-down stool, use insert panels for top and bottom.

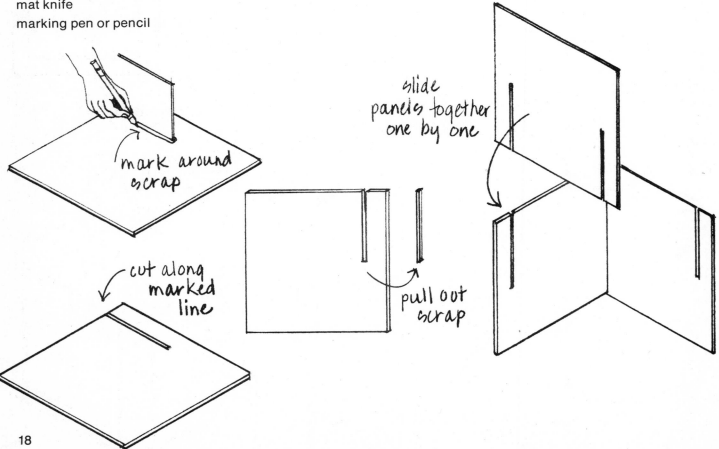

mark around scrap

cut along marked line

pull out scrap

slide panels together one by one

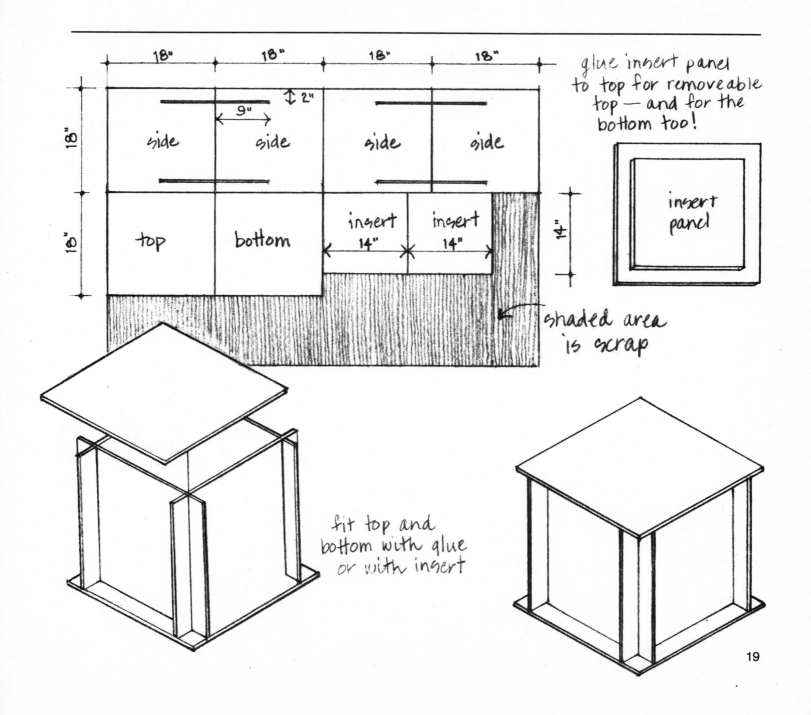

18" · 18" · 18" · 18"

18"

9"

↕ 2"

side · side · side · side

18"

top · bottom · insert 14" · insert 14"

14"

glue insert panel to top for removeable top — and for the bottom too!

insert panel

shaded area is scrap

fit top and bottom with glue or with insert

Fiberboard barrel chair

Materials

fiberboard barrel, 24″ diameter or bigger

¾″ plywood circular insert

2″ foam cushion

two dozen 1″ brass round-head screws

brown paper

fine sandpaper

masking tape

acrylic enamel and brush

marking pen or pencil

mat knife

screwdriver

For small children, a 24″ barrel will be big enough, but older children and adults will need larger seats. Make a template of the seat back on brown paper, cut it out, hold in place on barrel, and draw around it. Then cut away excess with mat knife and sand smooth. Tape cut edge before painting.

2″ foam cushion cover with a bright fabric!

3/4″ plywood is screwed to barrel

screws hold insert in place

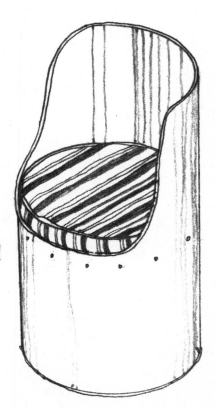

Floor foams

Small children love to sit on the floor, and teenagers, too, tend to prefer it, especially in school situations where tables and desks smack of ten-minute quizzes and other forms of torture. Perhaps this is their way of saying: "Look, I'm ready to listen and talk, but down here like this I won't be expected to write anything, will I?"

Buy some foam pieces, stack them thickly, cover with fabric remnants (canvas duck is best), and staple with staple gun to double- or triple-wall corrugated. Try single seats, odd-shaped scrap hunks, and love seat doubles. Toss in the closet when not using.

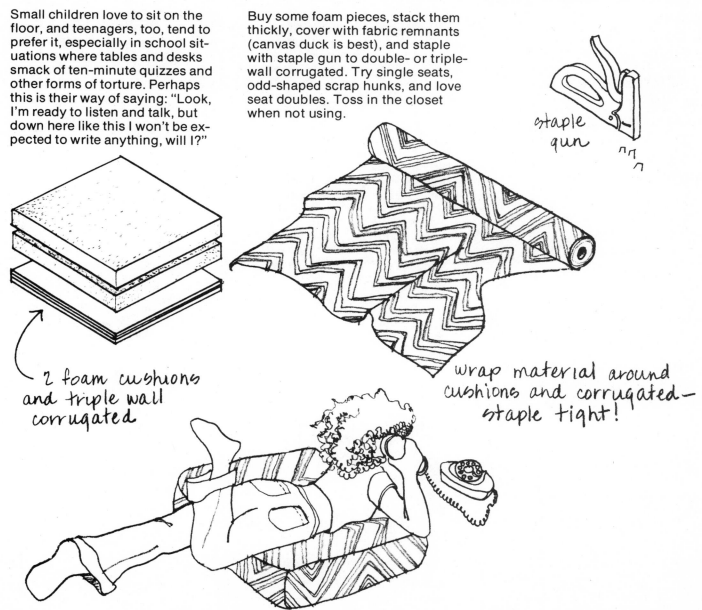

staple gun

2 foam cushions and triple wall corrugated

wrap material around cushions and corrugated— staple tight!

Slot-back chair

Materials

double-wall corrugated, *or* one sheet triple-wall corrugated for back, 48" × 72"

contact cement

masking tape

acrylic enamel and brush

mat knife

ruler or other straightedge

marking pen or pencil

This slot-and-assemble chair is made with a double back. All kids lean back in chairs, and the double back is a must if you want to keep chair and child from toppling over. Important construction detail: the rearmost slots in the side pieces must be cut double width so they can hold the two layers of double-wall corrugated or one of triple-wall that form the back support. Since the two backs slot into single-width sides, they should have the same width slots. You can use double-wall corrugated for child's chair, but chairs that will be used by adults or in schools (where they will get heavy use) should be made with triple-wall.

Measure and mark all pieces, then cut out with knife. Try slots for snug fit. Insert back pieces *one at a time.* Cement seat down and tape all cut edges. Prime and paint.

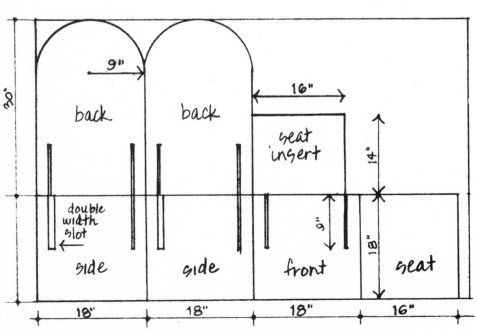

seat insert glued to seat make back edges even!

seat

back back seat insert side side front seat

30'

9"

16"

14"

9"

18"

double width slot

18"   18"   18"   16"

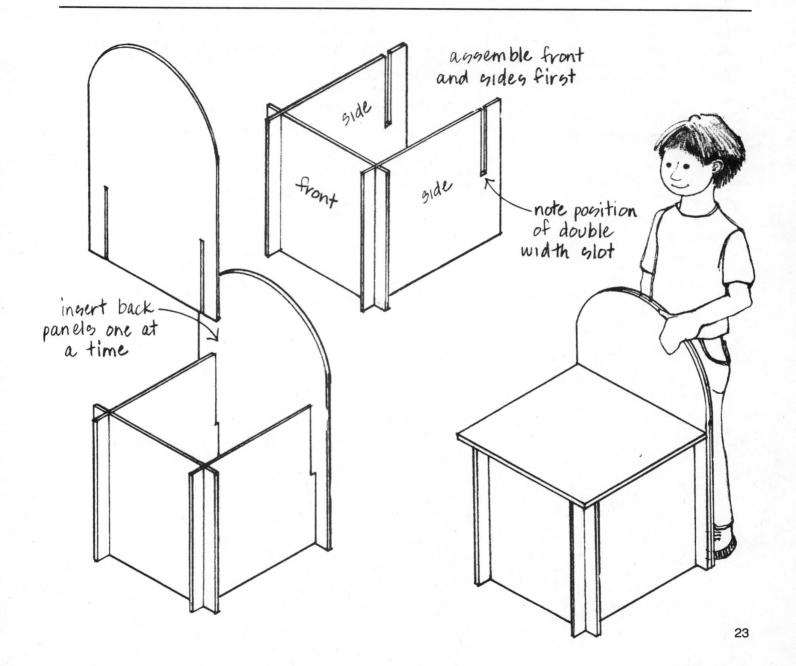

assemble front
and sides first

side

front

side

note position
of double
width slot

insert back
panels one at
a time

Triple-wall lounger

Materials

three pieces triple-wall corrugated, 24" × 30", 32" × 30", and 22" × 30"; or ¾" plywood

masking tape

acrylic enamel and brush

two pieces foam, 4" × 22" × 24" (for seat). 2" × 17" × 24" (optional, for back)

ruler or other straightedge

mat knife

marking pen or pencil

fine sandpaper

electric saber saw (for plywood version)

One of the beauties of this lounger is that you can store it flat when it is not in use, and it takes only a minute to assemble. For adult comfort use cushions on the seat and back. You can usually buy foam cut to your specifications. Don't pay higher prices for extra thickness, just double or triple the thinner kind. A plywood lounger is heavier and stronger, but more expensive to make.

Mark and cut sides, using first piece as template for others. Mark and cut back and seat. Now measure, mark, and cut slots and slide pieces together. Tape and paint.

For plywood version, visit local lumberyards and buy up scrap ¾" plywood to fit your dimensions. Borrow or rent an electric saber saw and cut carefully. Then sand to eliminate splinters.

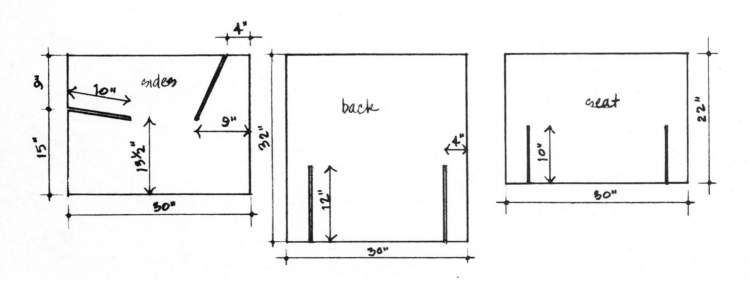

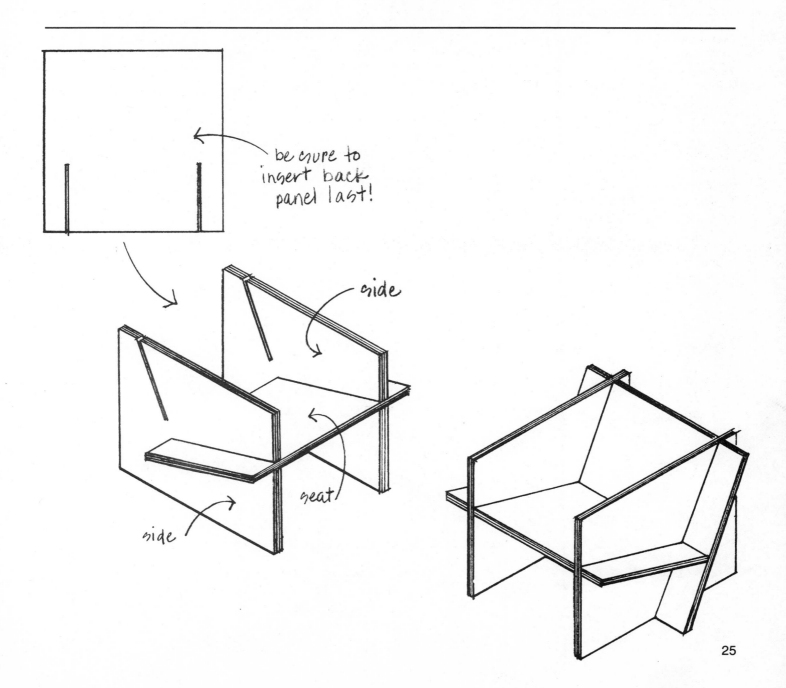

be sure to insert back panel last!

side

side

seat

Corrugated wing chair

Materials

triple-wall corrugated, 30″ × 48″ (for back, *must be one piece*), 15″ × 18″ (for seat), 15″ × 20″ (for brace)

brown paper (for template)

masking tape

acrylic enamel and brush, *or* fabric remnants and staple gun

4″ foam cushion (optional)

ruler or other straightedge

mat knife

French curve

marking pen or pencil

A "grown-up's" chair that can be executed in double-wall (for kids), triple-wall, and even quadruple-wall. The result is pleasing in shape, light, and very sturdy. It will provide greater comfort with 4″ thick foam cushions.

You will need to V-groove the corrugated back piece so that the corrugated will flex to right angles. This is a new technique, much like scoring—and easily mastered. The wing chair, like the lounger, requires no cement and will fold flat for easy storage.

Draw side template freehand or with French curve on brown paper and cut out. Lay on corrugated sheet and trace around. Allow 14″ for back, flip template over, and draw around template again, thus marking side A and side B. Measure and mark slots, side A and B. (If you are working with triple-wall, turn the sheet of material over and repeat the process just described to insure accurate cutting.)

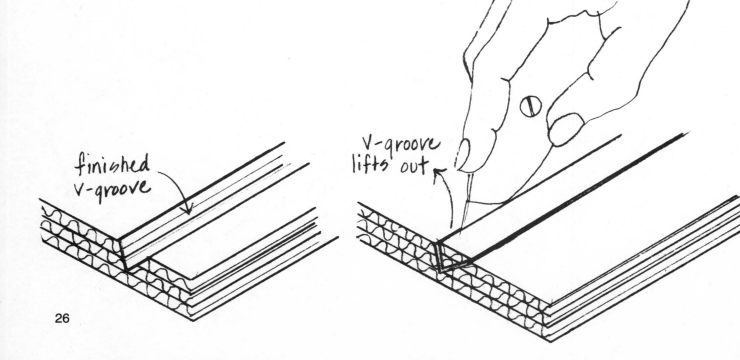

finished V-groove

V-groove lifts out

Now cut out side-A/back/side-B in *one piece.* Cut slots. Measure, mark, and cut out seat and brace. Cut slots in brace.

Before V-grooving, practice on scrap piece. If possible, use straightedge as a guide. V-grooves allow material to be flexed to 90° angle. Make two 45° cuts by holding mat knife at that angle. *Take care not to cut through corrugated.* Lift out V-shaped scrap and flex material. Try to make smooth, single slits with a single stroke. They should be about ¼" deep in triple-wall, ⅛" in double-wall.

When you feel you have the knack, V-groove back of wing chair. You will have better control when you cut toward you, from top to bottom. When you get to the middle, simply reverse piece and start again at edge. Corrugated should flex reluctantly after grooving, with plenty of stiff strength left. If

you cut too deeply and puncture the outside paper skin, repair with tape.

Assembly is simple. Fold in sides A and B so that seat tabs pass through slots. (Soap rubbed on tabs will help.) Trim, if needed, so that seat fits smoothly, flush against back and sides. Put chair on its back and insert brace. Trim so that chair stands evenly, without wobbling. Tape and paint or cover with burlap, which can be stapled and glued on. Wallpaper remnants can also be used to give the appearance of upholstery. For a very modern and elegant look, try Mylar, an exotic, chrome-finished plastic that is supple and quite strong, too. It will make your chair glitter like a mirror. Or why not use fake fur?

You can finish off your chair with fabric-covered foam cushions in complementary or contrasting shades and textures. This last touch will not cost much more money and will be worth it in eye appeal and comfort.

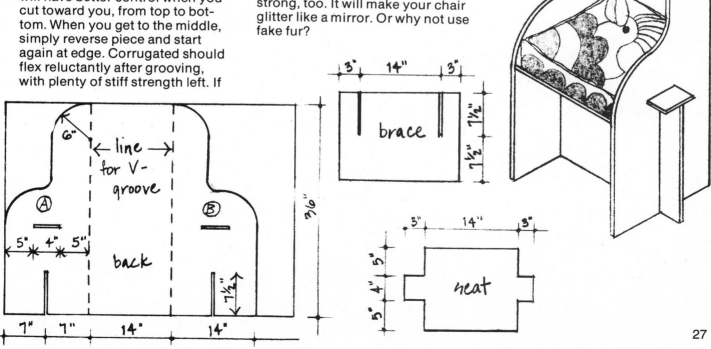

Basic tables and desks

Simple structures such as the ones illustrated here are nothing more than tops on bases. Tops can be made of triple-wall, ply-wood, chipboard or plexiglass. Always weight the base with sand. For a permanent structure, cement with epoxy or tape.

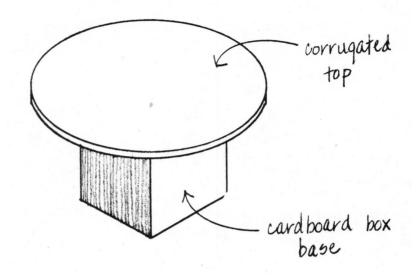

corrugated top

cardboard box base

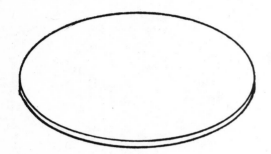

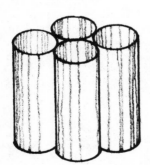

cement cardboard tubes in cluster for base

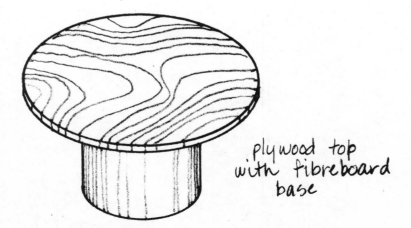

plywood top with fibreboard base

Stacked carton tables

Materials

two, four, or six liquor cartons of the same size, with divider inserts intact

sand

newspaper balls

contact cement

acrylic enamel and brush

precut tops of triple-wall, plywood, plastic, chipboard, plexiglass, or heavy-gauge metal

Liquor cartons held in clusters by contact cement, tape, or both can be combined with tops of various materials to make every size table from an end table to a dining room piece.

Pack newspaper balls between inserts for filler, and weight bottom cartons with sand for stability. Cement or tape cartons together as desired. Paint base and top and combine.

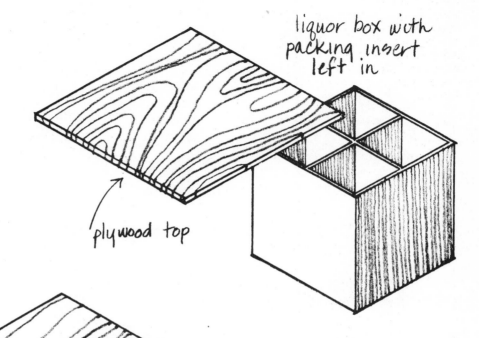

liquor box with packing insert left in

plywood top

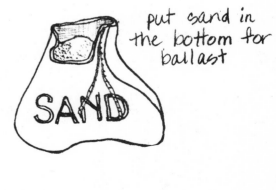

put sand in the bottom for ballast

SAND

tape or cement several liquor boxes together

31

X-brace coffee tables

Materials

two pieces triple-wall corrugated or ¾″ plywood, 28″ × 28″ (for base)

masking tape

sandpaper

acrylic enamel and brush

decorative self-stick paper (Contac, Mylar, etc.)

material for top: triple-wall, plywood, plexiglass, etc.

ruler or other straightedge

marking pen or pencil

saber saw (for plywood only)

string

nail

yardstick (optional)

drill (optional)

Low, strong, and stable, these tables should be made with ¾″ plywood or triple-wall corrugated *only*. Use decorative paper for fake-finished top.

Measure, mark, and cut out base pieces. Find midpoints and slot both pieces. Notch and cut away top of X-brace pieces to thickness of table top. Trim the bottom edges of X-brace pieces to create four small feet, so that table will stand without wobbling.

Making round tops for tables is easy. First, make your own compass with a nail, a length of string, and a pencil. Or sacrifice a wooden yardstick, drilling holes in it for a nail and a pencil. Of the two types of compass, the yardstick will be more accurate.

Obviously, you can cut tops out of various materials to fit an X-brace you have sized and constructed. Tops can be round, square, hex, or octagonal. For a permanent set-up, smear contact cement on the top of the X-brace, set the top in place, and let it dry. Then, tape and finish as desired. Left unglued, the top will pop in and out of X-brace, and the brace itself can be taken apart for storage.

For elegance, try a fake marble top (use marble-patterned Contact plastic sheeting). *Warning:* Contac "creeps" slightly and will not bond over masking tapes unless you take care to prime the tape that covers the raw edges of triple-wall corrugated. However, Contac looks great and adheres very well to untreated plywood and composition board. If you're using Contac, be sure to make slits along circumference for neat folding.

Another idea. Reversible top with acrylic enamel in a decorator finish on one side and blackboard paint on the other (for children to write on).

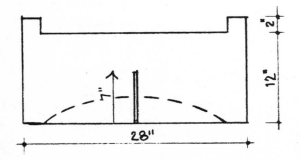

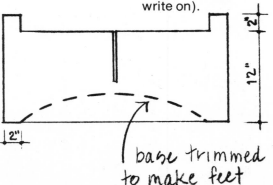

base trimmed to make feet

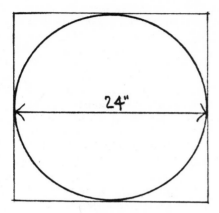

24"

making round
tops is easy!

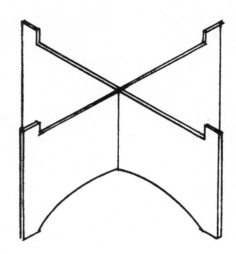

set decorated
round-top in
X-brace

2 easy ways to
draw a circle

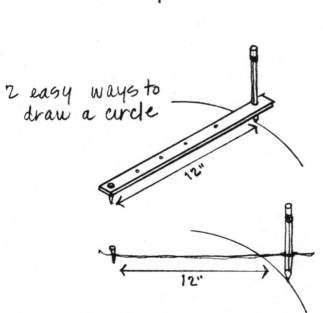

12"

12"

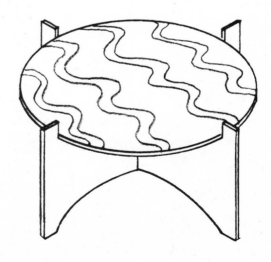

Five-piece desk

Materials

one sheet ¾″ plywood, 48″ × 96″, *or* triple-wall corrugated in dimensions shown on layout

fine sandpaper

masking tape

acrylic enamel and brush

marking pen or pencil

ruler or other straightedge

mat knife or electric saw (for plywood)

chipboard, 28″ × 57″

Since the sheets are large, you will most likely have to buy triple-wall corrugated or plywood to make this. However, the desk is a cinch to put together in a very short time, and it is almost impossible to make a mistake. The slots are 10″ on piece 1, 6″ on piece 2, and 4″ on piece 3. The only slots that are not of these lengths are found on the base of sides 4 and 5. Cut these slots 8″ long, and you will have a snug fit and a sturdy desk.

An unsupported length of 65″ for the top looks as if it might be weak and sag. The projecting flap, which rests on piece 2, prevents this, but to provide added support for a portable typewriter, drawing-board, or even elbows, have a 28″ × 57″ sheet of chipboard cut at a local lumberyard before you start building. This cover piece can be placed in position for instant work space.

Tape and paint the structure after assembly, but *do not paint piece 1.* No matter what you do, it will warp slightly. You can also cement the chipboard over it and add a very neat-looking metal trim along the edges if you wish. However, keep in mind that metal trim is finicky stuff to work with and must be measured very precisely. Be prepared for extra effort.

The best part of this project is the rapidity with which it can be completed. A rainy afternoon or post-lunch Sunday, and you're in business. But be sure to get that cover piece cut first. While you are making the desk, the kids can put together some stools using scrap materials.

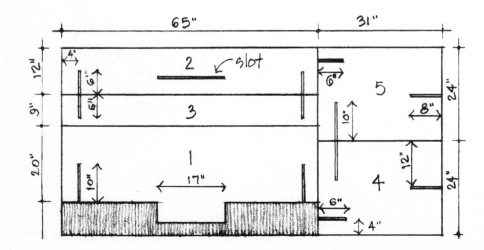

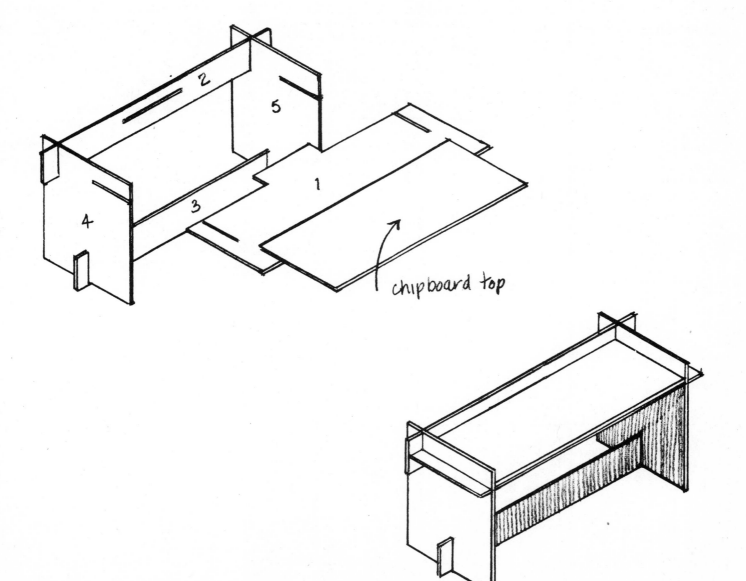

chipboard top

Triple-wall desk

Materials

two pieces triple-wall corrugated, 48″ × 72″, *or* ½″ plywood of same dimensions (follow dimensions given in layout)

two pieces triple-wall corrugated, 10″ × 30″ (for shelves)

ruler or other straightedge

marking pen or pencil

mat knife

masking tape

acrylic enamel and brush

saber saw (for plywood)

Lay out, measure, and mark all pieces as indicated. Cut out all pieces and cut slots carefully to insure firm fit. Assemble by sliding sides down on upright brace. Put desk on its back and slide in top. Slide shelves into positions. Tape and paint. (Incidentally, triple-wall is easily punctured with knives, pencils, even fingers. To avoid ruining furniture surfaces, shield them with old newspaper or composition board. You can also use plexiglass, but it will be expensive. All work surfaces should be smoothed with sandpaper.)

Companion pieces

With desk top set at 24″ from the floor, make a stool or straight-backed chair. (Cushion should be 18″ from the floor to provide ample leg room.) A second stool with removable top will serve as a storage or trash basket. Paint in contrasting or matching colors.

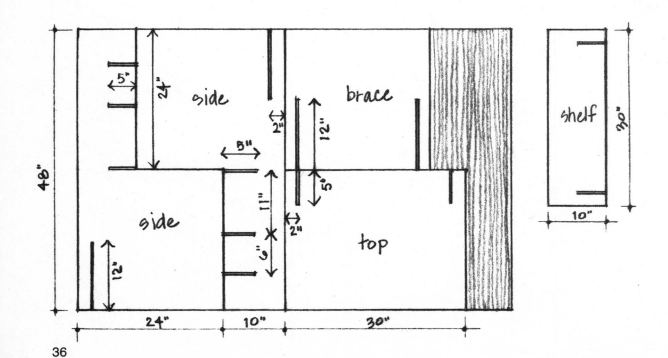

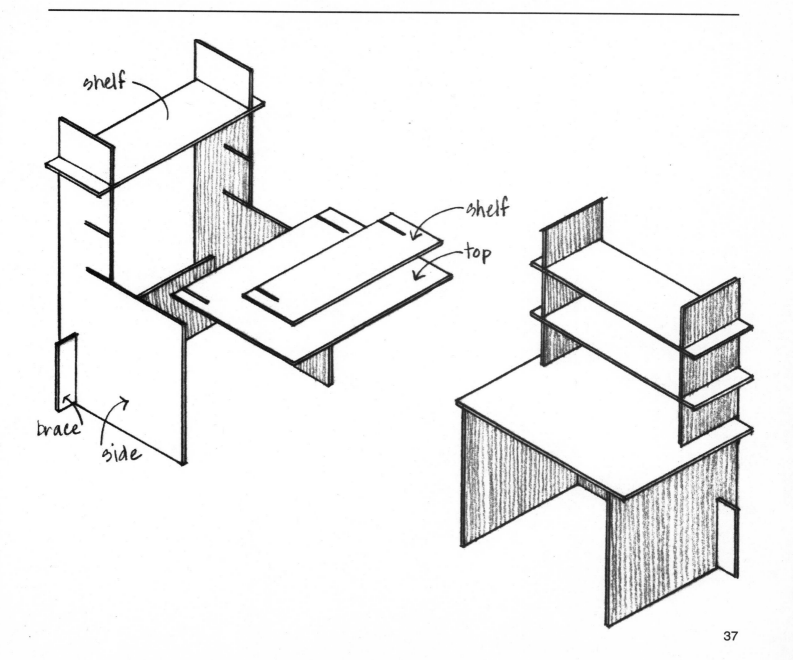

shelf

shelf

top

brace

side

Carton and door bed

Materials

five liquor cartons (with covers and divider inserts)

one hollow-core door (from nearest lumber yard)

sand

tape

acrylic enamel and brush

mattress (foam or regular)

contact cement

sandpaper

newspaper

Liquor cartons, a door, and a foam or regular mattress make a comfortable and cheap single bed. Each liquor carton can resist up to 400 pounds of crushing weight. The abrasive surface of sandpaper will hold door firmly, and there are no joints to work loose, no springs to sag. Bed is easy to make and can be stored in closet when not in use.

Distribute sand in bottom of each liquor carton and pack wadded newspaper balls between dividers. Tape on cover of each carton and glue on top of each, one sheet of coarse sandpaper (to retard skidding). Leave door unfinished to prevent mattress from skidding.

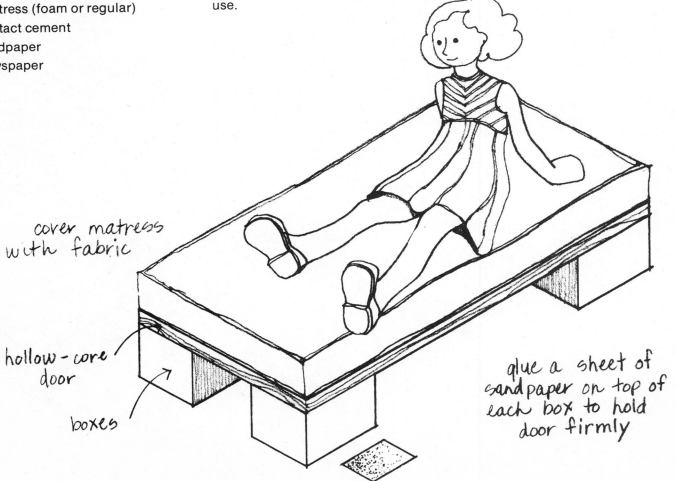

cover matress with fabric

hollow-core door

boxes

glue a sheet of sandpaper on top of each box to hold door firmly

Barrel bed

Materials

one 36" fiberboard barrel or mover's drum (new or slightly damaged)

two pieces triple-wall corrugated *or* ¾" plywood, 4" × 58" (for braces)

two pieces triple-wall corrugated *or* ¾" plywood 10" × 30" (for ends)

masking tape

acrylic enamel and brush

ruler or other straightedge

marking pen or pencil

mat knife

saber saw (for plywood only)

2" foam pad, 38" × 60"

Since you only need one-third of the fiber drum, measure, mark and cut away excess (for use on another bed). Now measure, mark, and cut triple-wall or plywood braces and ends. Slot and assemble. Tape and paint triple-wall, or sandpaper plywood. Glue foam pad in place.

A smaller barrel will make an infant's crib that is light in weight, easy to tote, and a cinch to assemble in seconds. Crib-bed will not tip over.

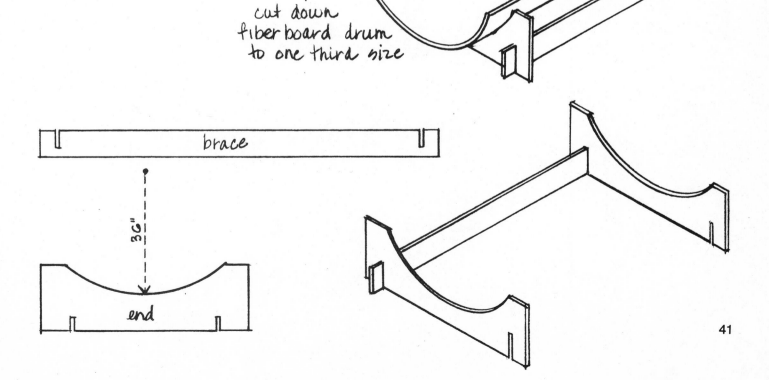

1/3

cut down fiberboard drum to one third size

brace

36"

end

41

Sleeping tube

Materials

one 36" fiberboard tube, 80" long

two pieces triple-wall corrugated *or* ¾" plywood, 4" × 72" (for braces)

two pieces triple-wall corrugated *or* ¾" plywood, 10" × 48" (for ends)

three pieces triple-wall corrugated *or* ¾" plywood, 8" × 30" (for insert)

one piece triple-wall corrugated, 72" × 36" (for mattress board)

mattress, foam or regular

contact cement *or* three dozen 1" brass, roundhead screws (for plywood only)

sandpaper

tape

acrylic enamel and brush

ruler or other straightedge

marking pen or pencil

mat knife

saber saw (for plywood only)

Order fiberboard tube from a commercial supplier (check the Yellow Pages). Sandpaper rough edges, cut a service window, and sand the edges. Measure, mark, and cut end pieces and braces. Test fit and trim after assembling so that edges are flush. Disassemble.

Stand tube upright; center on material for insert. Mark and cut out six inserts (see p. 45). Trim and sand for smooth, flush fit. Cement or screw at each end and in middle.

Now measure width of positioned insert. This is the lower width of mattress board. Allow 1" on each side for bevel and trim sides of mattress board to fit contours of tube. Cement or screw to insert for permanent set-up, if desired. *(Note:* Bevel is not necessary if you're using plywood, but looks neater and more professional.)

Tape or sand edges of ends and braces. Assemble paint inside and out. *(Note:* ¾" plywood will support a 4"-thick foam mattress.)

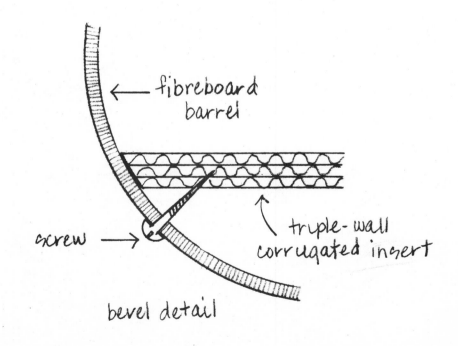

fibreboard barrel

screw →

triple-wall corrugated insert

bevel detail

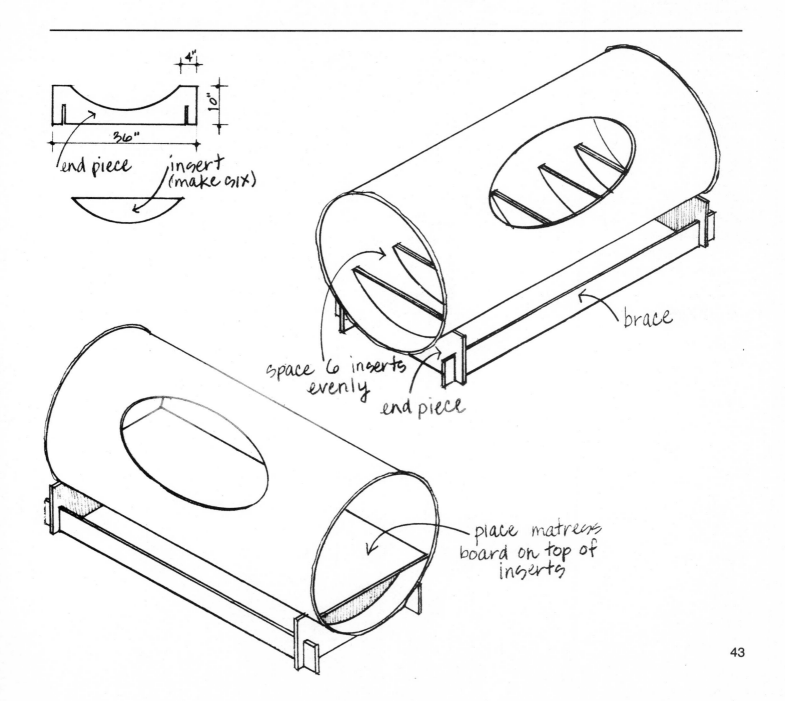

4"

10"

36"

end piece

insert
(make six)

brace

space 6 inserts
evenly

end piece

place mattress
board on top of
inserts

43

Sleeping tube bunks

Materials

two 36" fiberboard tubes, 80" long

two ¾" plywood sheets, 48" × 48" or 48" × 96" (for ends)

four pieces ¾" plywood, 6" × 72" (for braces)

six pieces triple-wall corrugated or ¾" plywood, 8" × 30" (for inserts)

two pieces triple-wall corrugated, 36" × 72" (for mattress boards)

two mattresses, foam or regular

contact cement or six dozen 1" brass, round-head screws

sandpaper

acrylic enamel and brush

1 quart wood filler

ruler or other straightedge

marking pen or pencil

mat knife

saber saw

This design *must* be executed in ¾" plywood. Wide base of panel end pieces with rigid bracing makes bed sturdy and safe. It will not tip over.

Order fiberboard tubes from a commercial supplier. (Oversized ¾" plywood can be obtained from manufacturers of industrial skids and shipping platforms.) Measure, mark, and cut out end pieces with saber saw. If you're using 96" plywood sheets, cut down. Sandpaper rough edges for flush fit.

Measure, mark, cut, and slot braces. Assemble with end panels, insert tubes, and adjust for flush fit. Disassemble and cut out windows in tubes. Sandpaper rough edges to smooth.

cut all pieces from 3/4" plywood!
extra strength is needed for this project!

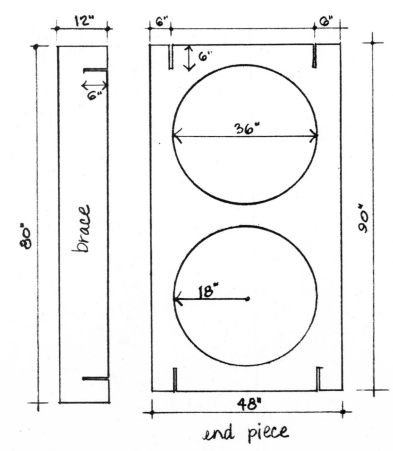

end piece

44

Stand one tube upright; center on material used for insert. Mark and cut out six inserts. Trim and sand smooth for flush fit. Cement or screw inserts at each end and center of both tubes. Measure width of insert. As before, allow 1" on each side of mattress boards for bevels. Trim mattress boards and cement or screw to inserts for permanent set-up, if desired.

Sandpaper edges of ends and braces. Apply wood filler to edge surfaces and sand smooth. Assemble and paint entire structure as desired.

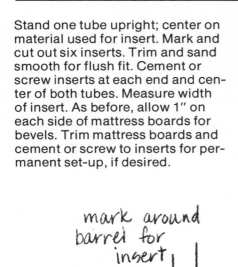

mark around barrel for insert

**remember to cut 1/8" inside marked line!

measure across circle for finished insert dimension

28"

finished insert

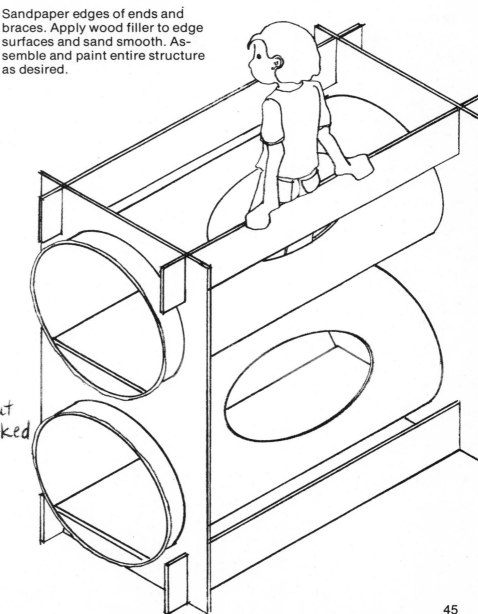

45

Triple-wall bed

Materials

three sheets triple-wall corrugated, 48″ × 72″ or 48″ × 96″

masking tape

filament tape (optional)

thirty-six pieces ⅛″ dowel, 4″ long

acrylic enamel and brush

6″ thick foam mattress (use single or layered pieces)

ruler or other straightedge

marking pen or pencil

mat knife

mallet or hammer

tools from Workshop for Learning Things (optional)

This slot-together construction with headboard and footboard held firm by dowels is simple to make and extremely strong. A 48″ × 96″ size is roomy for one, big enough for two. Bed knocks down for easy storage.

Measure, mark, and cut out pieces A-L. Measure, mark, and cut slots in A-J. Assemble as in layout. Tape all *exposed* edges only on pieces F-J, and tape *all* edges on pieces K and L (headboard and footboard).

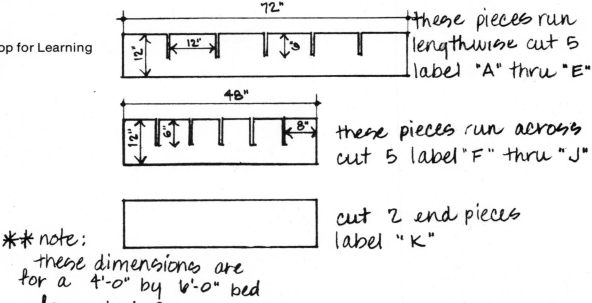

these pieces run lengthwise cut 5 label "A" thru "E"

these pieces run across cut 5 label "F" thru "J"

cut 2 end pieces label "K"

** note:
these dimensions are for a 4'-0" by 6'-0" bed
for a bed 8'-0" long pieces "A" thru "E" must be 8'-0" long
cut 2 additional 4'-0" pieces and label "K" and "L"

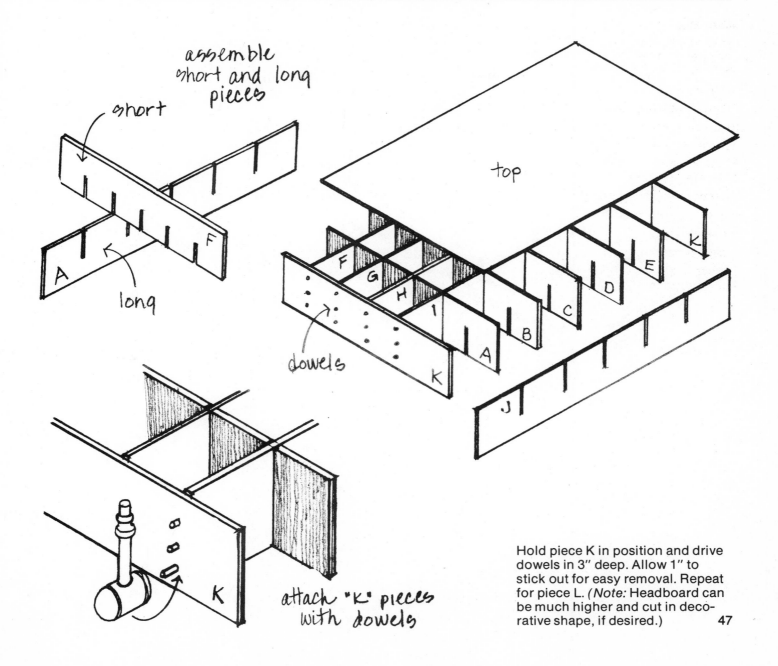

assemble
short and long
pieces

short

long

top

F
G
H
I

A
B
C
D
E

J

K

dowels

attach "K" pieces
with dowels

Hold piece K in position and drive dowels in 3″ deep. Allow 1″ to stick out for easy removal. Repeat for piece L. *(Note:* Headboard can be much higher and cut in decorative shape, if desired.) 47

Tape all edges of single-piece top.
For a hinged top that stores easily,
tape pieces together to fit with filament tape. Paint exposed pieces
as desired. Dowel top to frame.
Add mattress.

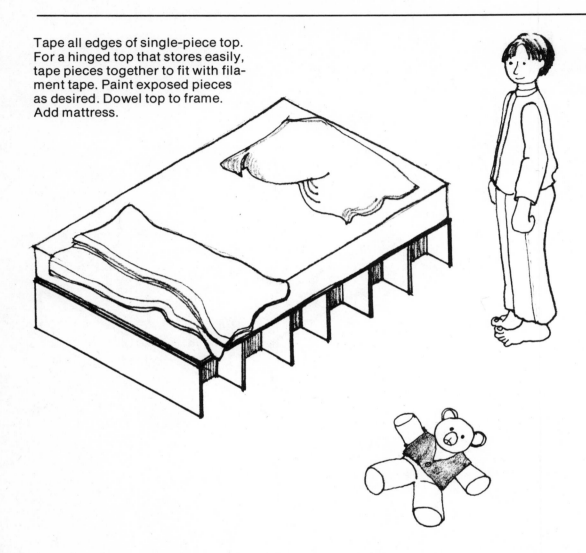

Storage units

Carton combinations

Materials

liquor cartons in ½ gal. and gal. sizes

wine cartons, all of the same size

contact cement

strong tape (3″ duct tape or 1½″ masking tape)

scrap iron inserts

scrap plywood, chipboard, etc.

plastic dishpans (optional)

cutting board (optional)

This system provides cheap, sturdy bookcases, storage walls, bureaus, and dressing tables. Do not try to stack cartons above a height of 48″.

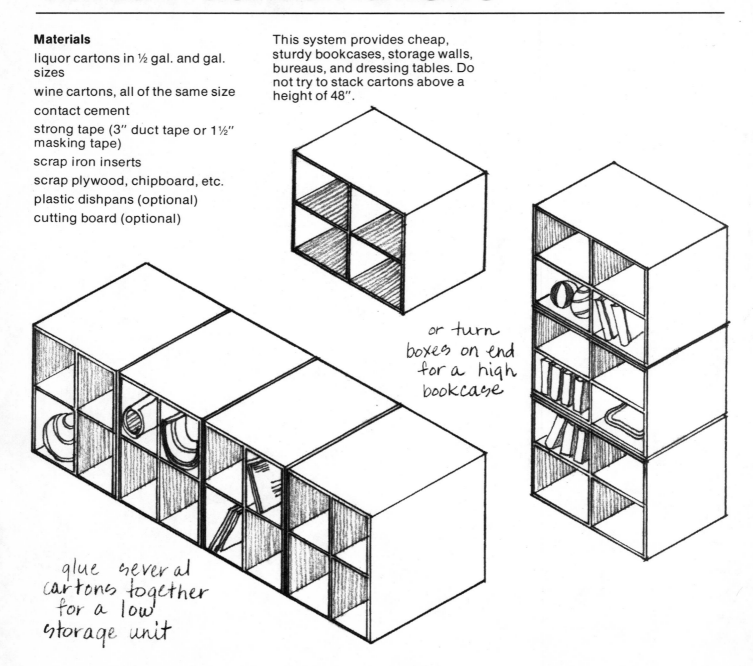

or turn boxes on end for a high bookcase

glue several cartons together for a low storage unit

Cement and/or tape cartons together in desired combinations
and heights. Weight lowest, inside
shelf with scrap iron plate. Tape
exposed edges. Paint or finish as
desired. (Scraps of plywood and
chipboard can be used for tops
and shelves between units. Use
plastic dishpans to make
"drawers.")

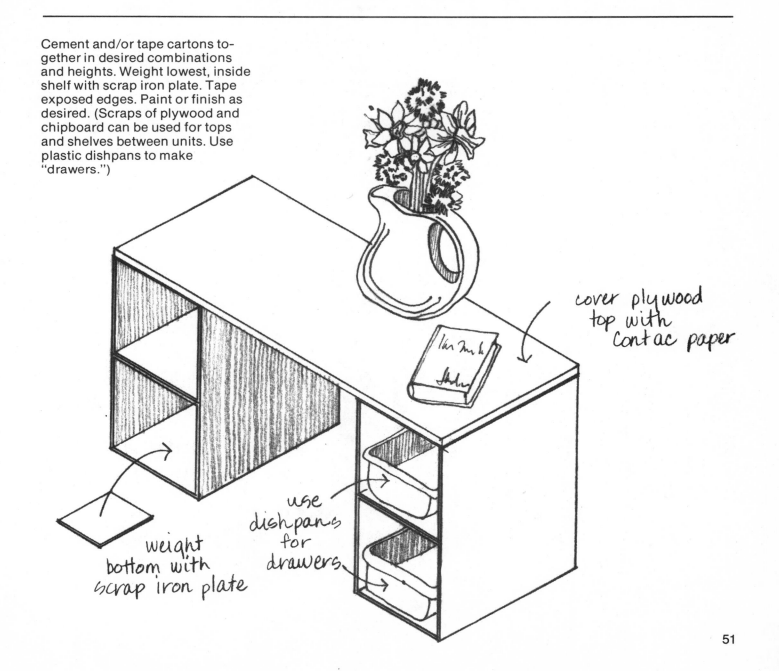

cover plywood
top with
Contac paper

use
dishpans
for
drawers

weight
bottom with
scrap iron plate

Triple-wall storage unit

Materials

same as for triple-wall bed (see p. 46)

Follow directions for layout and construction of triple-wall bed (change dimensions to suit). If you wish to build a temporary unit, slot together and dowel on sides K and L, then add back. For permanent assembly, use contact cement. Dowels here are optional, but will add rigidity to permanent structure.

Use common sense when stacking your storage unit. Do not overload it or stack heavy items on top shelves. Store books and heavy toys in floor slot and on two bottom shelves only. Shim front of unit to make it lean back against the wall.

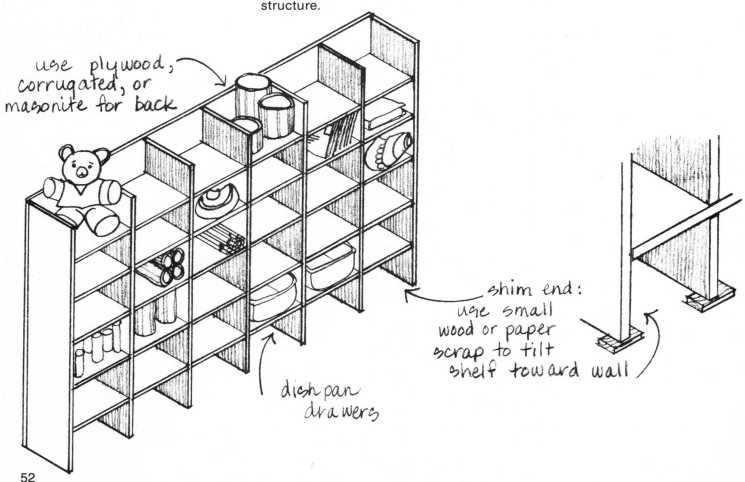

use plywood, corrugated, or masonite for back

dish pan drawers

shim end: use small wood or paper scrap to tilt shelf toward wall

Two storage units can be placed back to back and taped or cemented for a room divider. Face down, a storage unit with a back panel can be walked and jumped on, and it will provide instant theater-in-the-round in your living room or elsewhere. Children can play "raft," "space station," and other games of their own invention—so lay in some cartons, scrap cloth, and leftover Halloween masks. The kids will do the rest.

Simple play spaces

Carton creations

Combine a group of carton creations in contrasting colors. Tape. Why not add a roof?

Cut panels from big appliance cartons (triangle shapes are the strongest). Punch holes with a knitting needle. Lace together with plastic clothesline. Add odd-shaped doors and windows.

Create a play space, and you have made space for play. Salvage usable panels from damaged appliance cartons, cut out doors and windows, and tape panels together. Have the kids paint, paste, and decorate.

make a few simple shapes with paste and tape, or with rope and paint!

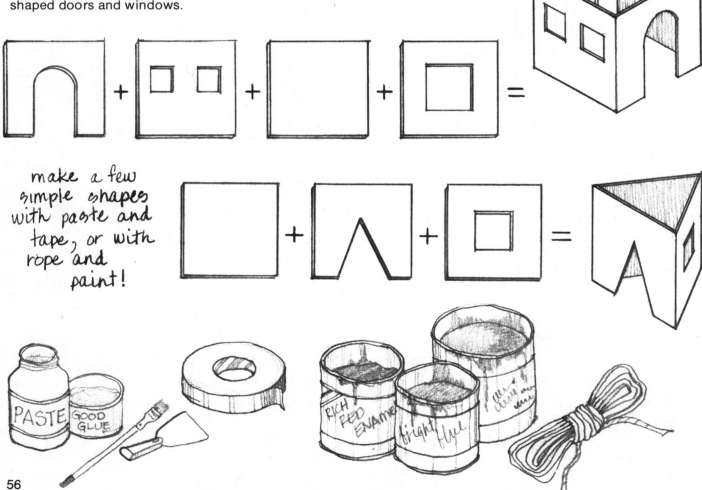

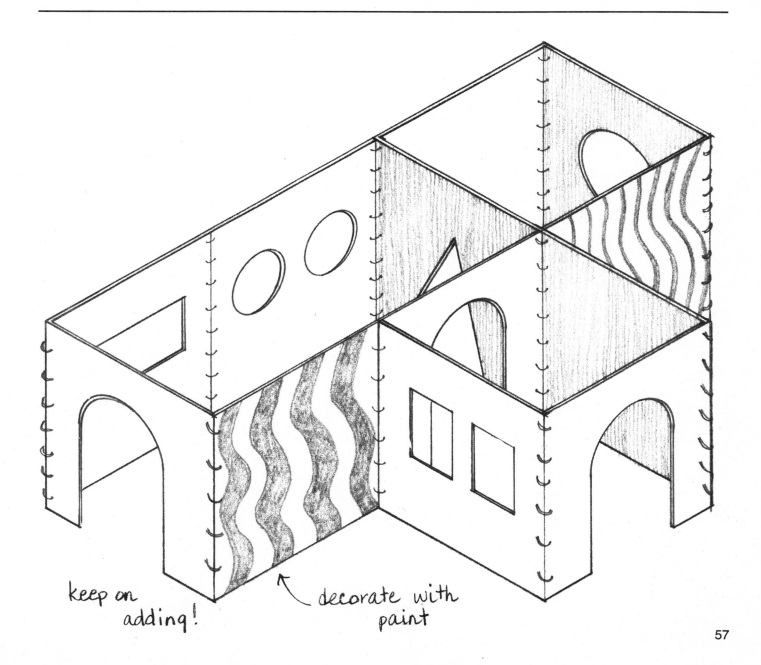

keep on
adding!

decorate with
paint

Panel play spaces

Mark and cut some matching panels from triple-wall or plywood.
Mark and cut out holes for fiberboard tubes (use tubes of standard diameter in different
lengths). Add some plywood or
hardwood planks and combine
tubes, triple-wall sheets, and
planks in whatever way you want.

any length!

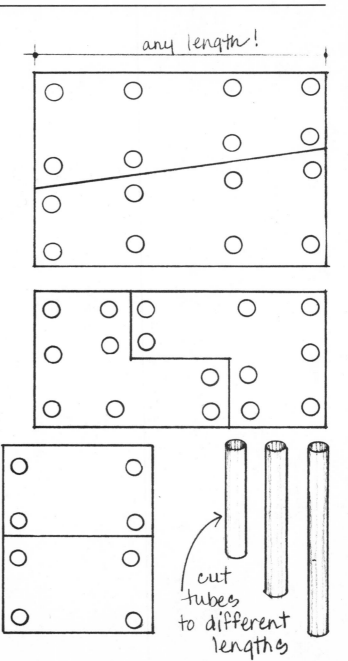

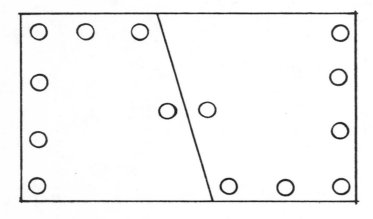

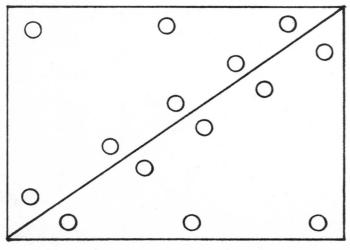

cut tubes to different lengths

You can make panel play spaces
for indoor and outdoor use—to
climb on, over, around, or
through.

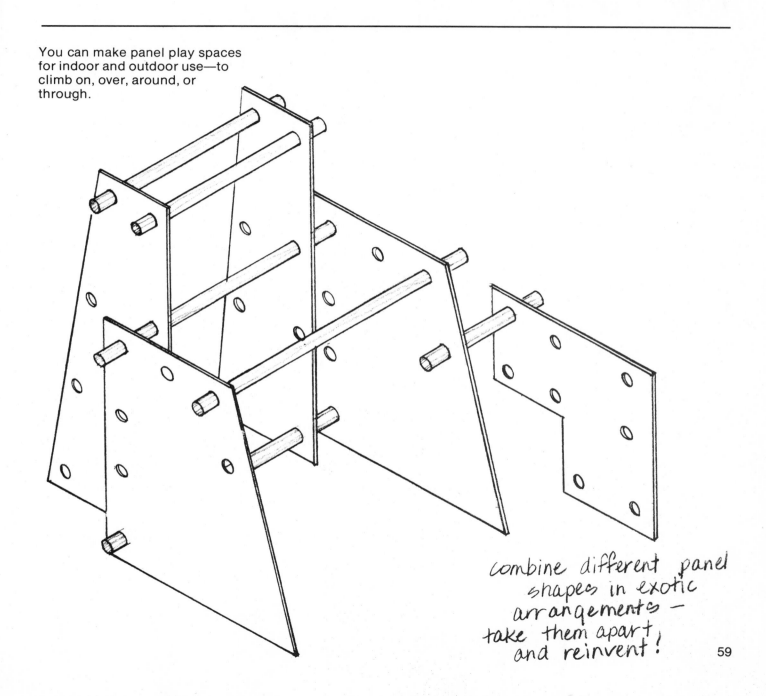

combine different panel
shapes in exotic
arrangements —
take them apart,
and reinvent!

59

Mini-sub

Before you impose too much realism on your constructions, stop to reflect that children are marvelously inventive. Make a play space look too much like the real thing, and you will be robbing kids of the chance to pretend it's something else. For example, one small city-dweller I know, after seeing the mini-sub, swarmed down the conning tower, closed the hatch, and began making noises like an air compressor. He was being "the man from Con Edison," installing new lines.

To make a mini-sub, take one 24" or 36" fiberboard barrel and cut a hole in side for entrance. Drill two holes, 8" apart, on each side and lace corrugated panel to each side. To complete sub, lace on more panels.

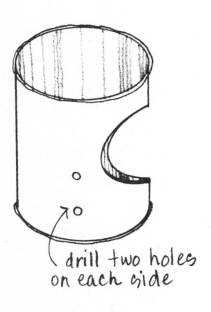

drill two holes on each side

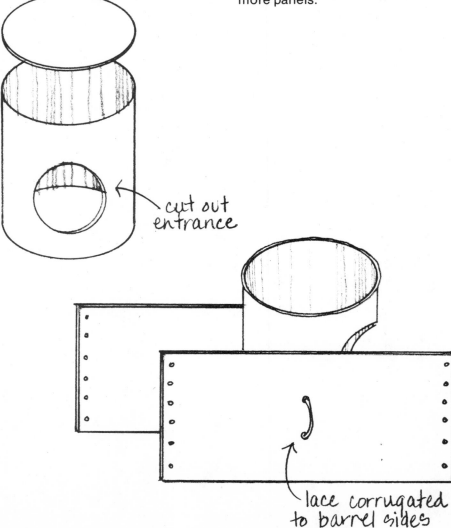

cut out entrance

lace corrugated to barrel sides

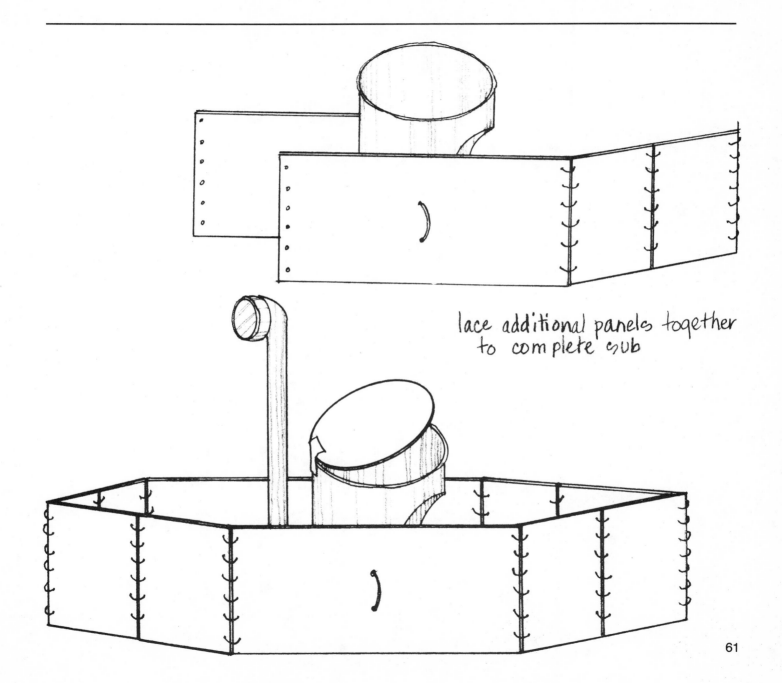

lace additional panels together
to complete sub

Castle or space station

For this play space, you will need three or more fiberboard barrels, some big sheets of scrap corrugated (scavenged from an appliance dealer), a sharpened dowel to make holes, and enough vinyl clothesline to lace it all together. Paint, and let the kids decorate with signs.

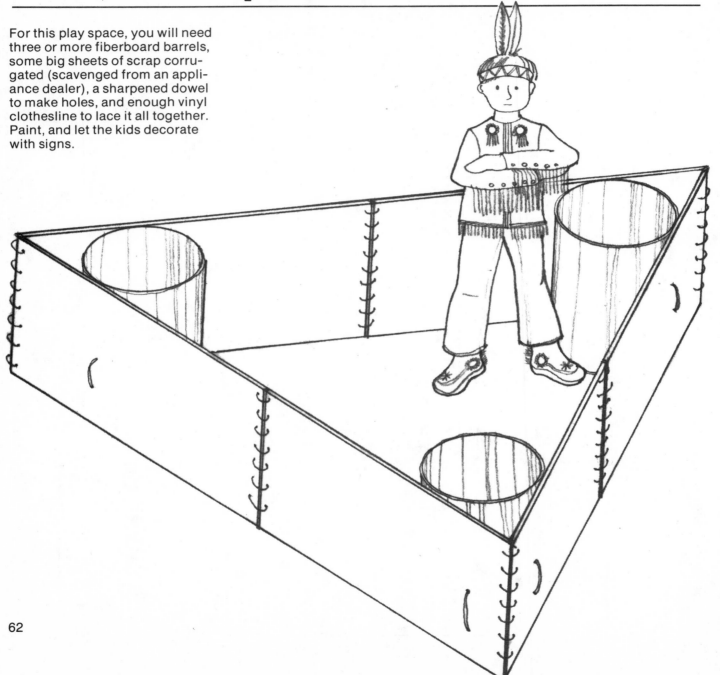

Monster mouths

A 36" fiberboard barrel can be painted to look pretty scary. Add a set of fangs made from sheet rubber or plastic (blood red, of course!), and it will look even more ferocious. Actually, as a secret place for reading, coloring, or just dreaming, a clean barrel with a foam cushion is great. It's very popular with dogs and cats, too.

Another idea. Combine a pair of barrels with a length of 24" fiberboard tube for a "squirm-through."

put a cushion inside for a comfortable house to sit in!

connect barrels and squirm through tunnel

3" foam cushion

Lacer-spaces

A lacer-space is by its nature a temporary structure. Kids will invent ways to change the shape as they are building it and after it is finished. And you can forget about neatness, perfect edges, taping, and paint jobs. All kids like to jump from the idea to the completed object, and they are usually impatient with what adults consider the pleasures of "a job well done." They just want it done—and the sooner the better!

assembled are correctly proportioned and cut evenly. Let the kids do the cutting with a pistol-grip handsaw, not a mat knife. Then show them how to use the lacer-jig. Provide plenty of lacing material and get out of their way.

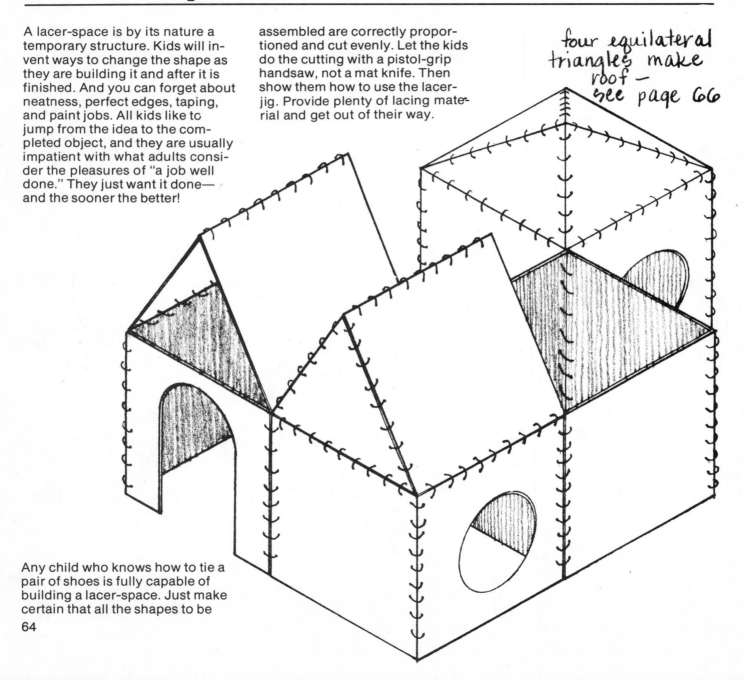

four equilateral triangles make roof — see page 66

Any child who knows how to tie a pair of shoes is fully capable of building a lacer-space. Just make certain that all the shapes to be

64

How to make 'em. Triple-wall is the best type of corrugated for making lacer-spaces, but for things like roofs you can use double-wall (salvaged from cartons) or combine different thicknesses of materials. Avoid plywood or masonite, however, because these materials are too heavy for small children to manipulate. And their great joy is movement—of objects and themselves!

Holes can be drilled freehand or using the lacer-jig as a guide. If you think you're going to be doing a lot of building, a lacer-jig is worth the effort. Make it of light wood, nailed or glued together. Holes should be set back ¾" from the edge to prevent corrugated from ripping. The ideal space between holes seems to be about 4" (but a little less is ok, too). If kids are using the lacer-jig, just explain to them that they place it over the edge of a shape and drill *all* the holes before removing it. Remember: The fun of the lacer-space is how fast you can build it.

Use plastic (vinyl-covered) clothesline for lacing. It is very easy to work with—stiff enough to push through holes, yet flexible and smooth. Small fingers can tie knots in it, but it will not jam or shrink when damp, the way hemp or manila does.

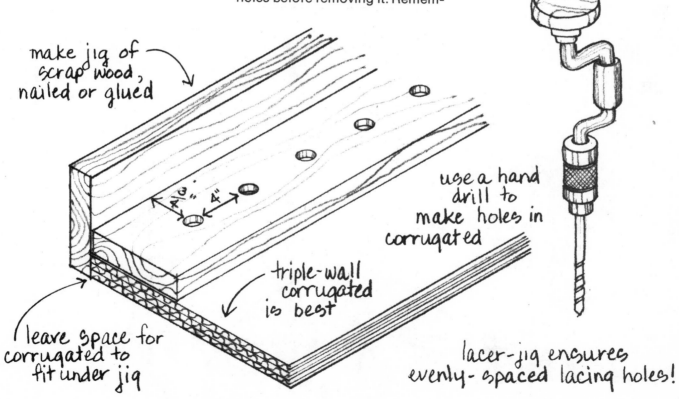

make jig of scrap wood, nailed or glued

leave space for corrugated to fit under jig

triple-wall corrugated is best

use a hand drill to make holes in corrugated

lacer-jig ensures evenly-spaced lacing holes!

Some helpful hints. To make a perfect equilateral triangle, measure your base with a string and a pencil, then strike arcs of the same length. Mark sides with a straightedge and cut. Before lacing shapes together, make a knot in your lacing material to prevent slipping. Thread lace through a washer, and knot.

For more lacer-space ideas, look at geoshapes, pp. 96-110.

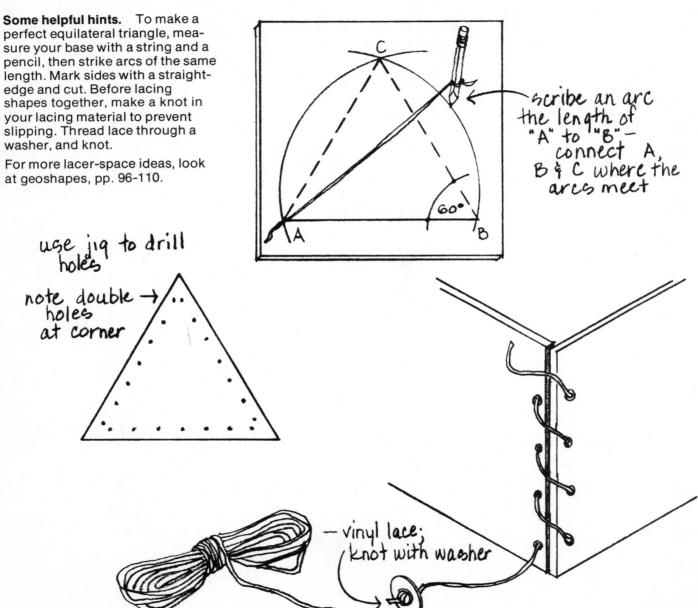

scribe an arc the length of "A" to "B" — connect A, B & C where the arcs meet

use jig to drill holes

note double → holes at corner

— vinyl lace; knot with washer

Tents and domes

Although some of the constructions in this chapter may at first glance look complicated, they are not. Most of these play spaces are combinations of equal sides and equal angles. Simple and amazingly strong, they can be assembled by children as well as adults.

Complex trigonometric formulas have been omitted here, and the directions are not always too specific. Experiment and you will get some idea of what the kids can do. Making models is a good idea—these will occupy children during any slack time between initial concept and finished project. Test out your own ideas, too, and get a good sense of the combinations possible. For models, use construction paper, soda straws, Saran-wrap, glue, pins, etc.

If you pay a visit to your local lumberyard (check out scrap and bargain bins), new design and building possibilities will also open up to you. However, don't buy anything you don't need—lumber and other construction material can be very expensive. Instead, scout for scraps, remnants, and junk. (Remember to check on barn or garage sales listed in the local paper.)

Try to keep structures simple, unspecialized, and not too finished—the right combination of the cheap, the commonplace, and the useful. And remember, no matter what you say, once a kid sees a structure that *can* be climbed on, he *will* climb on it. Cover all doweled structures pronto. Unless you are handy with fabrics or plastic sheeting, use old newspaper sheets and quick-setting glues. Newspaper sheets are wide, and they can be overlapped and trimmed easily. Newspaper can also be strengthened and waterproofed with a quick spray coat of shellac. When the kids poke holes in a construction, all you have to do is patch it with more paper. And when they get bored, you can slit the paper away, scrub off the residue, and use your materials to make another play space.

Standard sizes are used throughout for materials listed. Coupling systems (see Appendix) are available at hardware stores and lumberyards, and although these may be expensive, they can be used and reused.

Triangle house

Materials

fifteen pieces single-wall corrugated, 30″ × 30″ or 40″ × 40″

sixty 3/16″ bolts, 1″ long

sixty wing-nuts to fit bolts

120 washers, flat, to fit bolts

ruler or other straightedge

marking pen or pencil

masking tape

acrylic enamel and brush

mat knife

mudge-tool

If you're making the house for very young children (up to five years of age), you can cut corrugated panels 24″ square. For older children, make 36″ panels.

Make panel template using ruler and protractor to measure the 60° angle. Score with mudge-tool and punch holes in flaps. Lay out template on other corrugated sheets and cut out remaining panels. Punch holes for bolts and score flaps.

Flex scored flaps. Trim off excess on flaps so that panels can be joined easily. Assemble play space on the floor, starting with the roof and working down. Arrange panels 1 through 5 with flaps facing *up*. Bolt together. Add other panels, working from center out. (*Note:* There is no panel between 6 and 7. This is the crawl-door.)

When house has been assembled, turn it over, tape edges, and paint. Bottom flaps not connected to other panels can be taped or cut off.

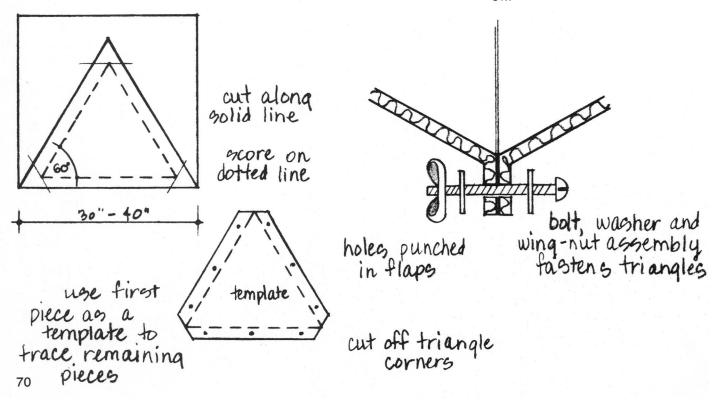

cut along solid line

score on dotted line

30″ – 40″

use first piece as a template to trace remaining pieces

template

holes punched in flaps

cut off triangle corners

bolt, washer and wing-nut assembly fastens triangles

60°

70

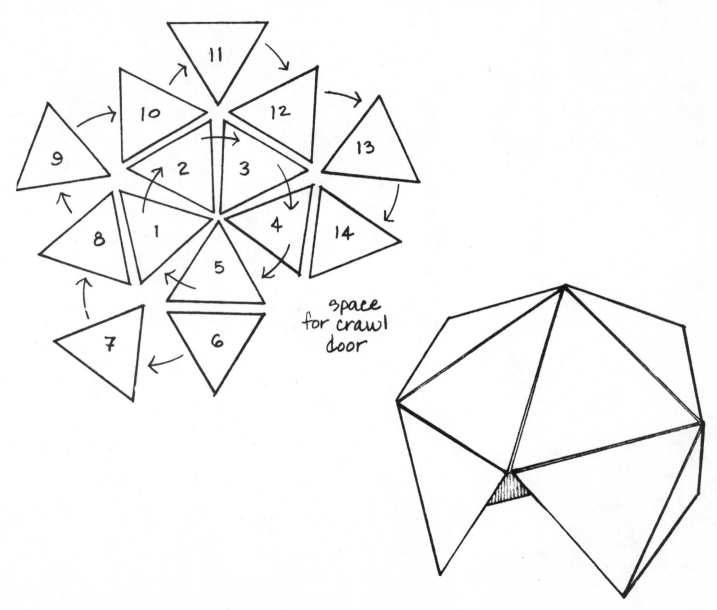

space
for crawl
door

Penta-hex dome

Materials

sixteen pieces of single-wall corrugated, at least 24" square

six dozen 3/16" round-head bolts, 1" long

six dozen wing-nuts to fit bolts

144 washers, flat, and 144 bolts

mat knife

ruler or other straightedge

protractor

marking pen or pencil

cutting board

1" masking tape

large knitting needle

mudge-tool

air conditioning tape, 3" wide

Six corrugated pentagons bolted to ten corrugated hexagons make a simple Fuller-dome play space for small children. Dome is about 5' in diameter and 3' high at center, with crawl-door. It stores in the closet.

All sides on the pentagon and hexagon shapes in the dome are the same size (12"), but naturally, the angles in the hexagon are greater (120°) than the angles in the pentagon (108°). They must be figured accurately, so study work plans before beginning. Check dimensions and angles carefully before cutting out the templates.

Construction hints. A simple no-fail method for making pentagons is shown here. Draw circle on material. Draw diameter through center and divide into five equal parts with ruler. Set compass at width of diameter and scribe arcs from each point on diameter. Now draw line from arc through point 6, as shown. Draw line from point 6 to point 1 and set your compass at this length. This is your pentagon side. Mark around circle from point 1 and connect points.

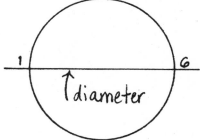

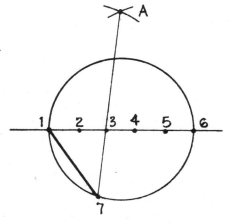

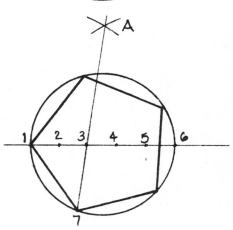

Another method for making pentagons is as follows: draw a 12" line roughly parallel to one edge of a sheet of corrugated board. Beginning at one end, with protractor, plot a 108° angle, draw another 12" line, plot the next angle, and so on until you return to the first line, thus completing your pentagon.

To make a hexagon, select a sheet of corrugated board and mark a line 12" long approximately parallel to one edge. With protractor, plot 120° angle at one end of this first line. Mark off another 12", plot another angle, mark again, and so on around until you are back to the first line, completing your hexagon.

Now, to make pentagon and hexagon templates, allow 2" flaps with corners angled, as shown, to avoid overlaps and bindings. Cut out and make relief holes (for bolts) with tip of mat knife. *(Note: Bolt holes must be evenly spaced for easy joining.)*

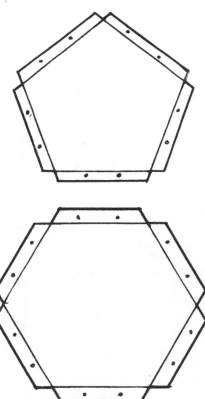

pentagon template with angled corners and relief holes

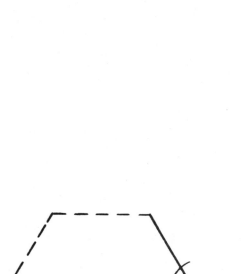

Making the dome. Make a total of ten hex panels and six penta panels. Cut, angle corners on 2″ flaps, and score each flap with mudge-tool (one side only). Make relief holes and fold flaps.

Place a penta panel with *flaps up* on the floor. Set five hex panels on floor, flaps up. (See p. 77 for arrangement.) Now, bring flaps together, score lines *inside,* and hold for flush fit. Pierce relief holes with knitting needle. Insert bolts, washers, and wing-nuts.

Do not tighten wing-nuts. You will note as you bring the flaps together, the panels must be permitted to flex slightly.

Once you have attached the hex panels to the first penta panel and the upper-side flaps of the hex panels to each other, you will see at once where the remaining penta panels attach to hex panels. *No penta panel is bolted directly to another penta panel.* Punch holes and proceed with bolts, washers, and wing-nuts.

Now, bolt remaining hex panels to the base flaps of the first rank of hex panels and lower-side flaps of the penta panels. (Once you have fastened the first set, the rest will be easy.) Finally, tape those flaps that form the base and turn the whole dome over. The kids will tighten any wing-nuts that need it.

When the dome is completely assembled, waterproof the panels inside and out to prevent warping. Buy a roll of 3″ wide air conditioning tape from a wholesale dealer, and when the panels are dry, seal all the seams. Cover all surfaces that will touch the ground with this tape, too. You may also wish to raise the base above ground level to further protect dome. To raise, staple the base flaps to wood blocks or scrap plywood pieces.

You can paint the panels in contrasting colors or in two shades of the same color if you like. I don't recommend this, however, since kids typically write on the panels or cut out pieces for windows. Remember: Make the dome too fancy and you make it too much yours, not enough theirs.

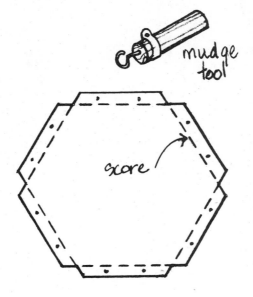

mudge tool

score

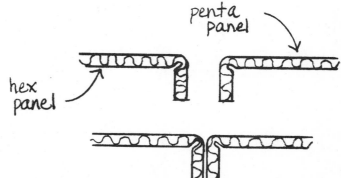

penta panel

hex panel

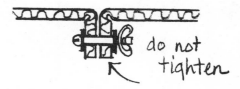

do not tighten

Note: Instead of bolting panels together, you can spray each flap with contact cement. This takes a steady hand, but it makes a neat dome.

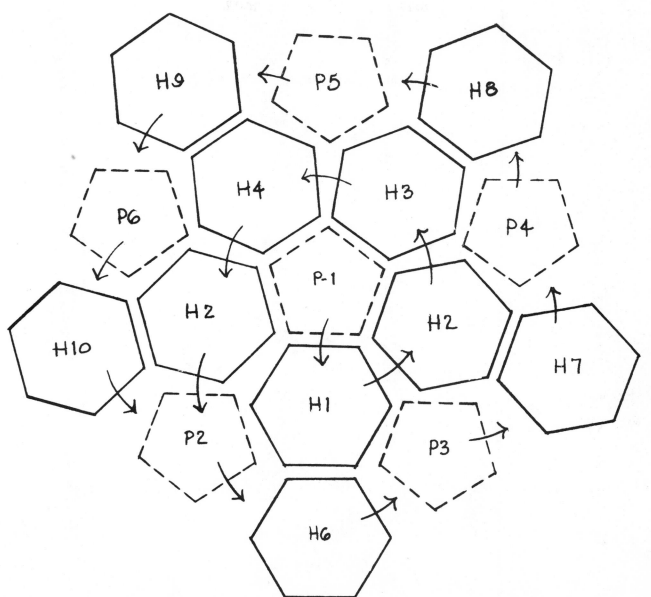

Dowel tent

Materials

one piece 2" × 2" select white pine, 6' long *or* four-way plastic pipe joints (see Appendix)

twenty-four pieces ½" dowel, 2' long

twelve pieces ½" dowel, 3' long

lightweight canvas duck (sail-cloth) in at least two colors (remnants are cheaper and will make more interesting tents). *Or* newspaper.

handsaw

drill with ½" bit

needle and heavy thread

This Tinker Toy-like structure of dowels and cube connectors is easy to make, inexpensive, and simple to store. Fun to play in, but not to climb on. It can be used indoors and out.

Cut pine into 2" lengths to form cubes. Make thirty cubes. Save scrap piece. Drill ½" holes on all six sides of each block; each hole should be about ½" deep.

Sandpaper tips of dowels.

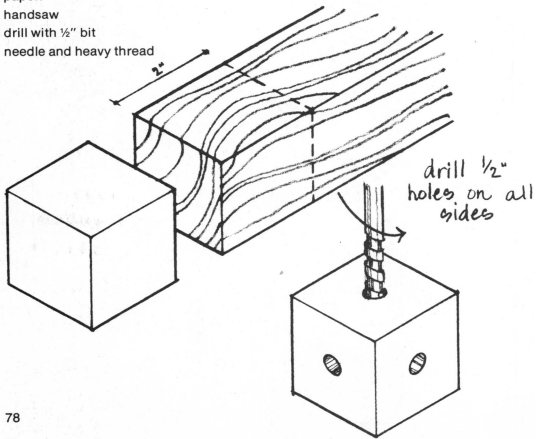

2"

drill ½" holes on all sides

Cut fabric into pieces 24″ × 26½″;
this allows 1¼″ at top and bottom
for hem. Sew to form squares.
Now cut some other pieces 24″ ×
38½″ (1¼″ hem at top and
bottom). Sew to form rectangles.

Slip dowels through hems in fabric and assemble dowels and
blocks.

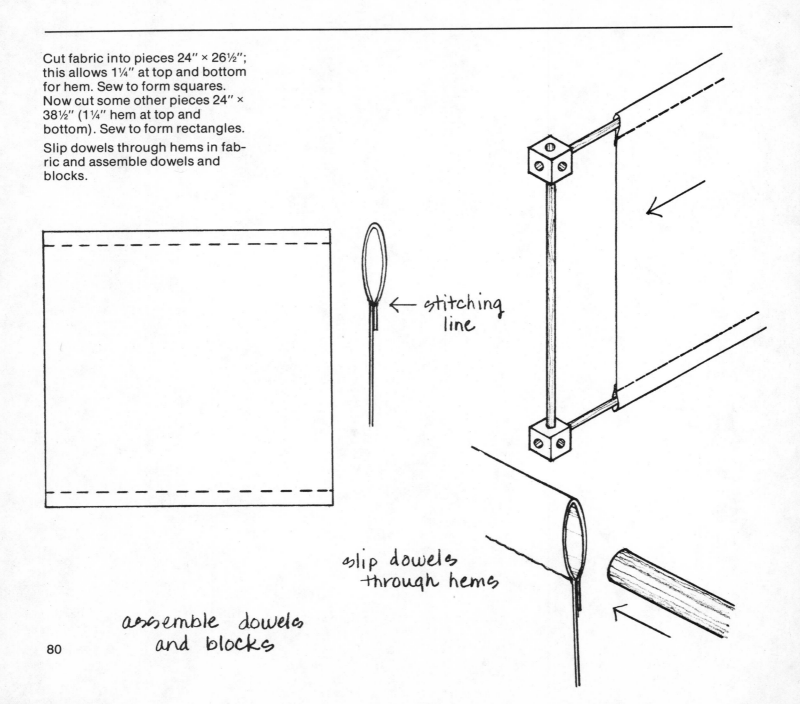

← stitching
line

slip dowels
through hems

assemble dowels
and blocks

Covering tent with newspaper. If remnant canvas runs into too much money for you, there's a perfectly adequate alternative— newspaper.

Overlap sheets of newspaper and glue together. Then trim pages to needed size, allowing for a "hem" at top and bottom. Apply quick-drying cement along edge and fold over a dowel. Smooth and pull taut. Glue bottom hem and fold up. Now spray with shellac or plastic to strengthen and waterproof.

With newspaper, each room has pictures to look at, cut out, punch out. And the walls and roof can always be stripped off and discarded if you decide to cover the tent with something else.

Don't use plastic to cover the tent; it sags and stretches in the sun and will make both the grass and the kids "boil" in no time.

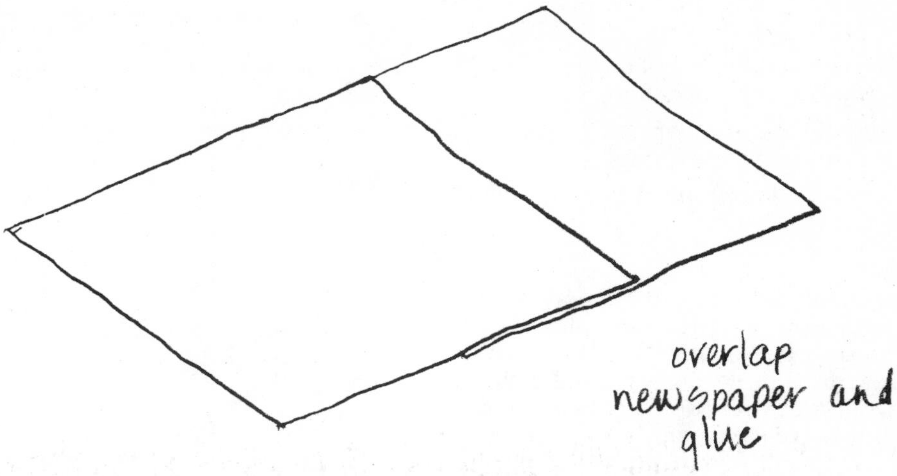

overlap newspaper and glue

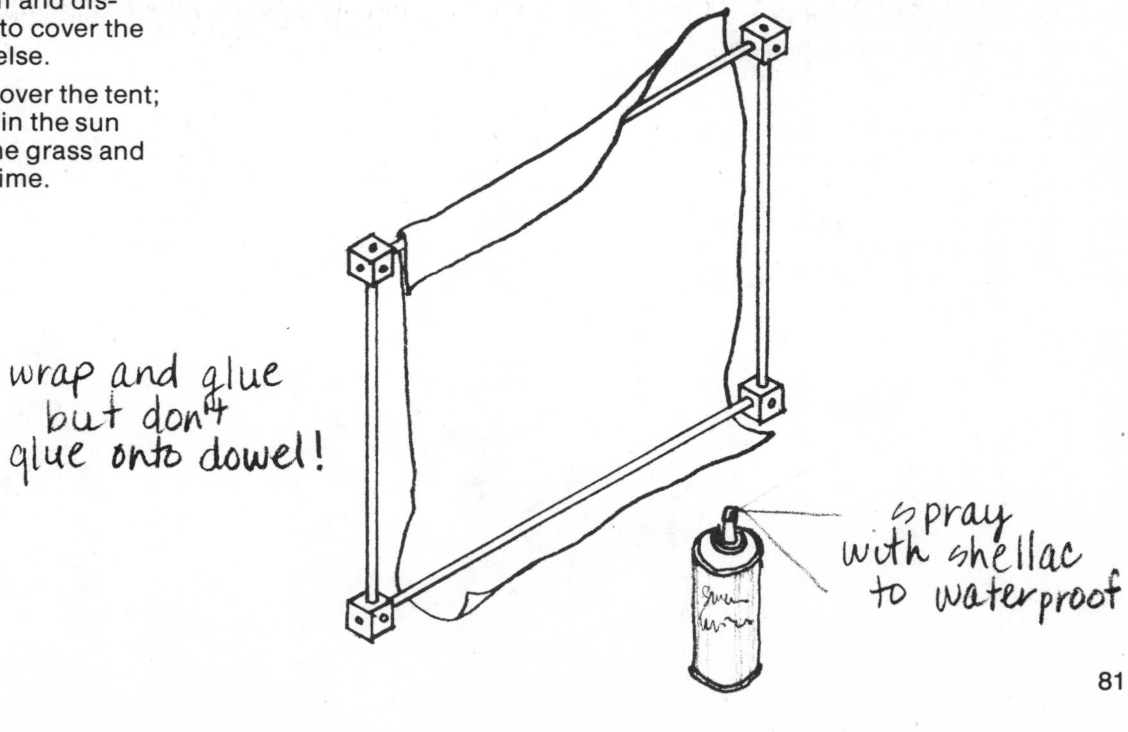

wrap and glue but don't glue onto dowel!

spray with shellac to waterproof

81

Garden hose tent

Materials

4" garden hose hubs (see **Construction hints**)

six pieces dowel to fit garden hose, 48" *or* 60" long

polyfilm sheeting *or* newspaper *or* single-wall corrugated

contact cement *or* rubber cement

tape

With hubs made from 4" sections of cheap plastic garden hose; bolts, nuts, and washers; plus a supply of ½" dowels, children can assemble three-dimensional play structures that can be crawled into *(but not climbed on!).*

Construction hints. To make garden hose hubs, cut plastic garden hose with a mat knife. Drill through each section of hose. Assemble as shown, using bolt, two washers, and wing-nut for each hub.

Standard ½" dowels should fit garden hose (inside diameter of garden hose is generally ½"). However, test to make sure dowels slide into hose. Fit should be snug but not too tight.

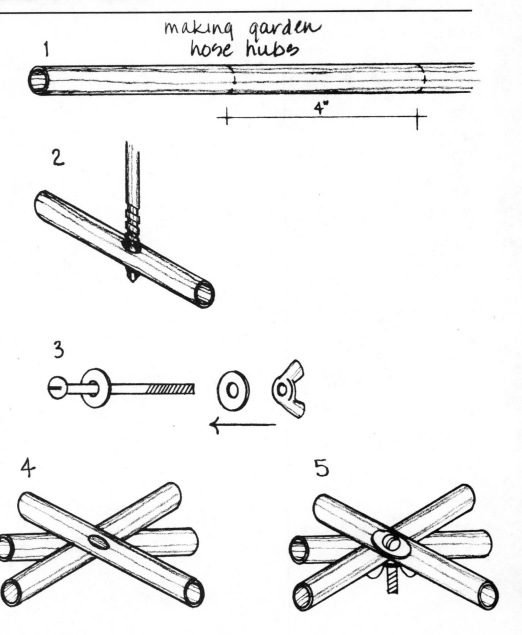

making garden hose hubs

1

4"

2

3

4

5

Building the Tent. Connect hubs A, B, and C with dowels. Plug dowels in hub D, bend, and plug into A, B, and C. *To cover tent if you're using newspaper:* overlap sheets of newspaper with glue, and wrap around dowels at top and bottom. Leave as is or spray with shellac.

If you're using polyfilm: tape instead of gluing.

Alternate construction: Cover tent with sheets of single wall corrugated. Lace tent sides to dowels with vinyl-coated clothesline.

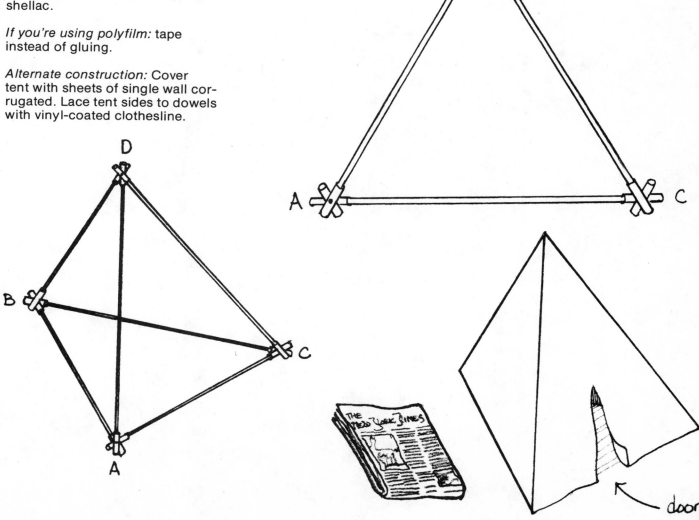

Garden hose dome

Materials

eleven garden hose hubs

eighteen ½" dowels, 3' long

heavy twine (optional)

material for covering (polyfilm, newspaper, etc.)

Again, *no climbing* on this play space. Dowels of this size easily break and splinter under the weight of even small children. Incidentally, before they build the dome, kids should experiment with some basic shapes by pushing dowels into assembled hubs.

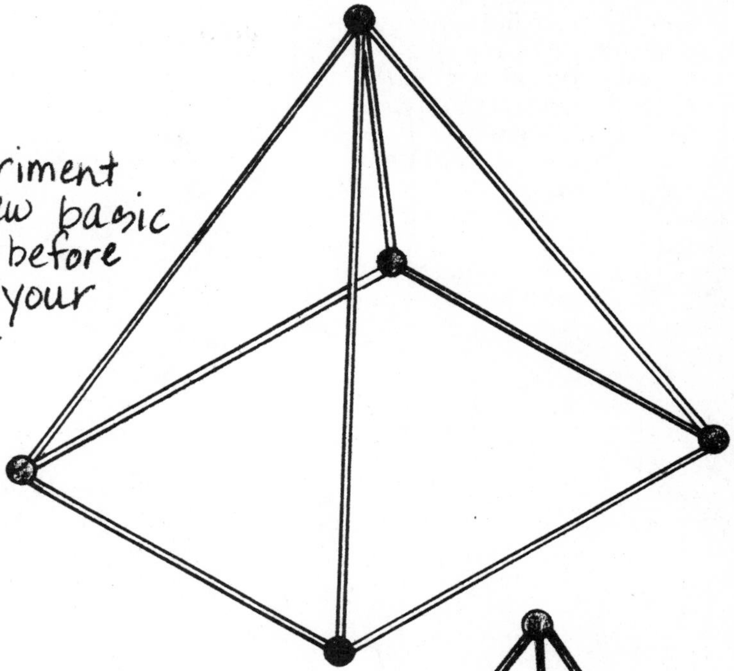

experiment with a few basic shapes before building your dome

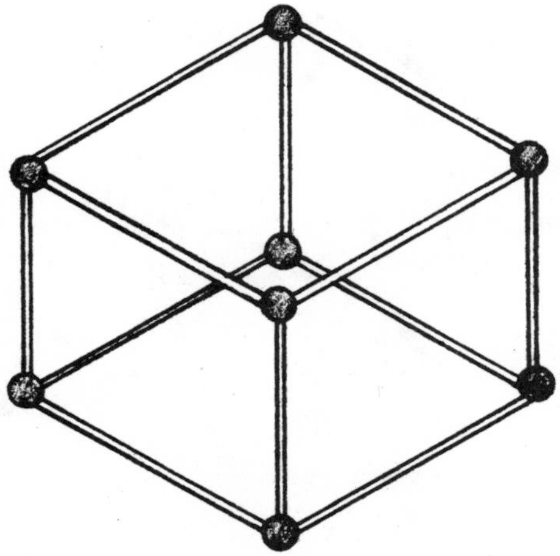

← gray circle represents garden hose hub

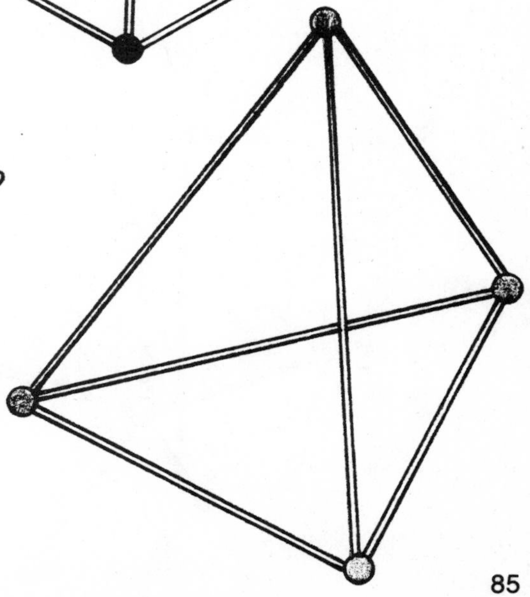

Building the Dome. Connect dowels and hose hubs in a pentagon pattern. (Why not take a felt-tipped marking pen and label the points as is done on the layout? This will make the rest of the assembly quick and easy.) Use two hubs set one atop the other in the center of the pentagon and connect them to points A, B, C, D, and E with five more dowels. Now position five more hubs at the points indicated so they can be doweled, too.

The next step is obvious. Points A and B are connected to V with dowels; points B and C to W; and so on. This step will be easier if someone—preferably an adult—takes a piece of heavy twine, wraps it around the central top hub, ties a firm knot, and lifts structure slightly off the ground or floor. Meanwhile, the kids can scramble around pushing the new dowels into hubs V, W, X, Y, and Z.

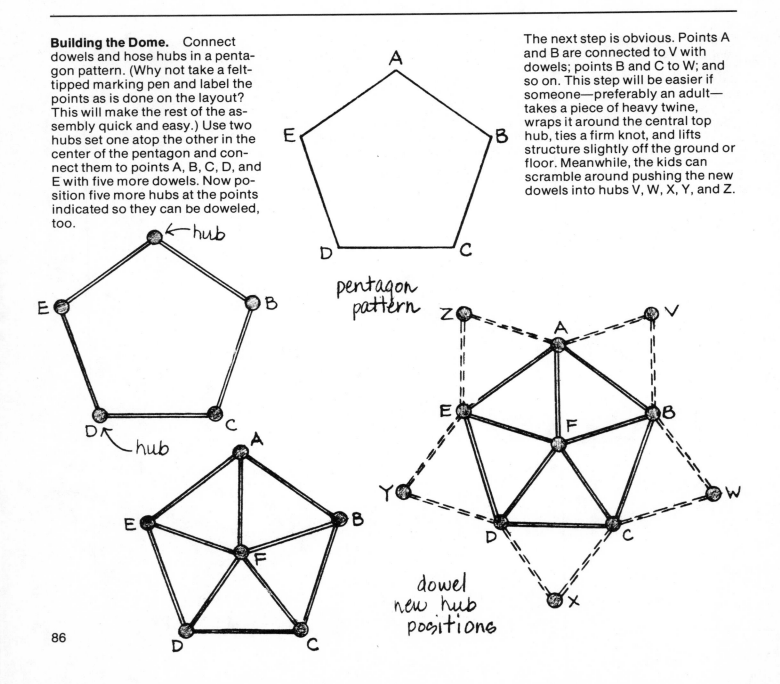

pentagon pattern

dowel new hub positions

This five-pointed star must be supported by someone until the engineers make it stable by using the remaining dowels to couple V to W, W to X, X to Y, and Y to Z. Finally, Z is connected to V. Two marvels: the kids have built a true icosahedron dome house (you only "helped"), and you have learned that this simple structure depends on the ability of the hubs to flex slightly. It will give before it breaks. It also weighs very little and stores in the bottom of a closet.

The kids are sure to point out that the dome could be bigger. Check costs first. You can go to 4' dowels. Or double everything: Use 1" plastic hose (or pipe), longer, thicker dowels, and 4½" bolts with corresponding washers and nuts. However, your span between hubs will be pretty long in this case. A better idea is probably the two-frequency dome (see p. 88).

Remember that your covering is really a safety feature as much as a protection. A polyfilm plastic dropcloth from a paint store will give you a light cover for very little money, but the plastic will make your dome hot and airless. Cut-out window vents should help, but a cheaper—and better—idea is the Sunday paper.

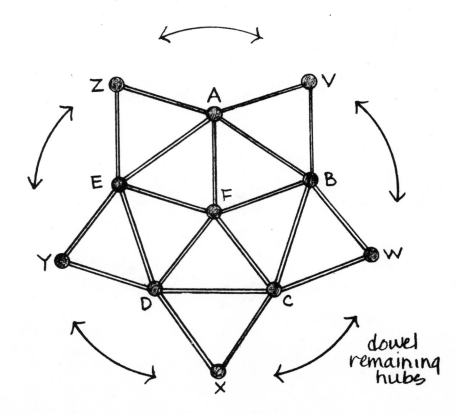

dowel remaining hubs

Two-frequency dowel dome

Materials

twenty-six garden hose hubs

thirty ½" dowels, 3' long

thirty-five ½" dowels, 31¾" long

colored marking pen or pencil *or* quick-drying paint

The ultimate in pint-sized domes. It is simply built of dowels and garden hose hubs, is big enough for a gang of kids, yet stores in a box and a paper bag. Cost? A mere $10 or $15—depending on how much you can scavenge. For construction, one adult is needed to hold up the dome while the kids build.

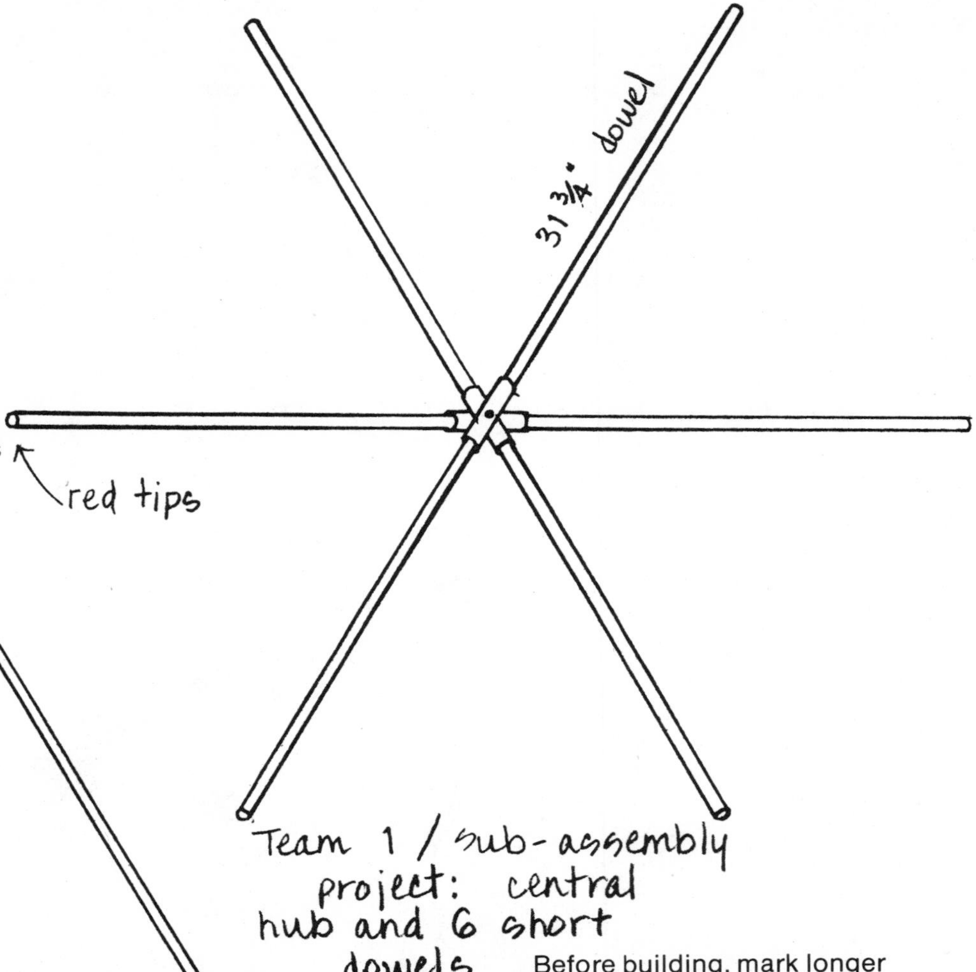

red tips

31¾" dowel

36" dowel

Team 1 / sub-assembly project: central hub and 6 short dowels

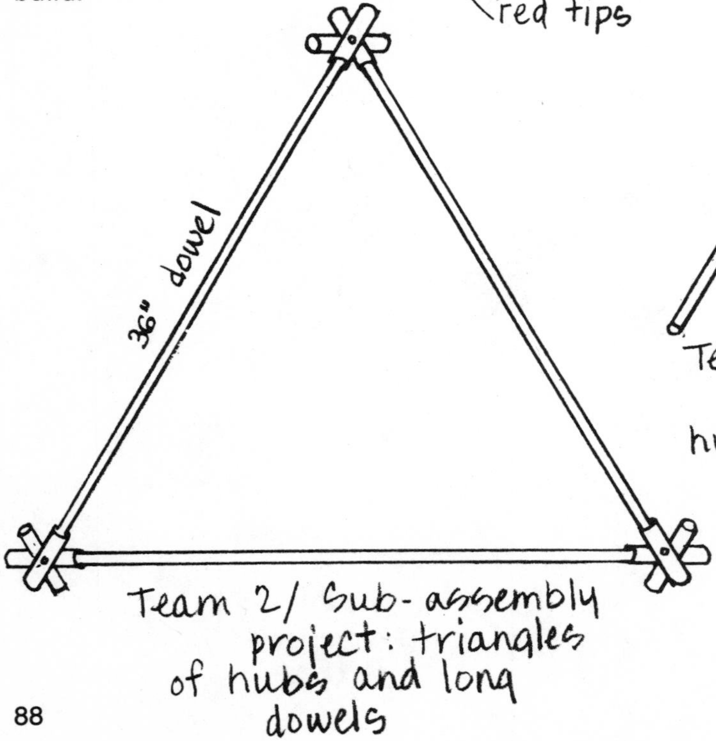

Team 2/ sub-assembly project: triangles of hubs and long dowels

Before building, mark longer dowels blue at both ends, and shorter dowels red. Now divide workers into two groups. Team 1 will make 9 triangles with hubs and longer, blue dowels. Team 2, stars with hubs and shorter, red dowels.

Follow diagram to subassemble. (*Note:* Some hubs are removed as new connections are made.)

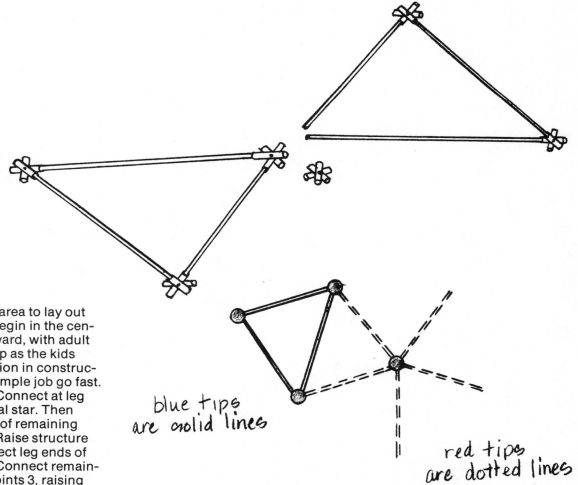

Now, find a large area to lay out subassemblies. Begin in the center and work outward, with adult lifting the dome up as the kids build it. Cooperation in construction will make a simple job go fast. Begin at point 1. Connect at leg ends of this central star. Then connect leg ends of remaining stars at points 2. Raise structure slightly and connect leg ends of stars at points 3. Connect remaining triangles at points 3, raising dome again. Push up and plug in base dowels at points 4.

Cover entire dome with newspaper for safety and strength. Spray with shellac to stiffen and waterproof.

blue tips
are solid lines

red tips
are dotted lines

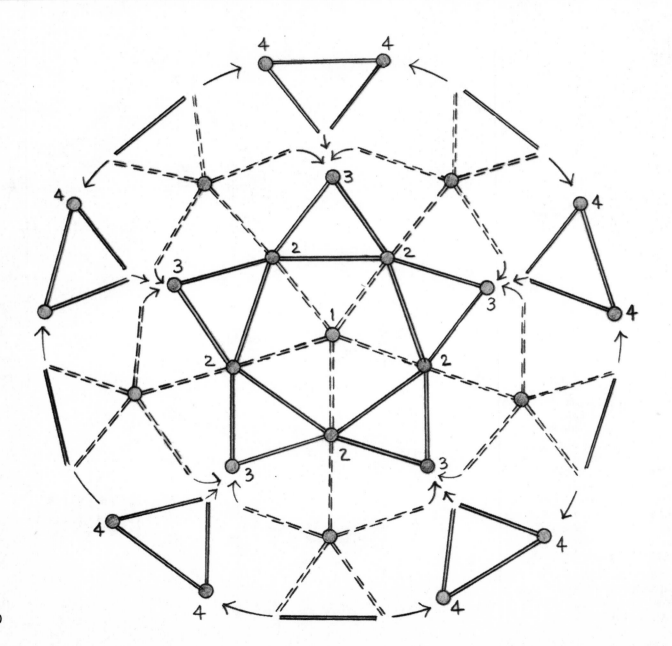

Inflato-spaces

Inflato-spaces

The first inflated structure I ever stood inside was a temporary gymnasium at a school in South Carolina—a huge, billowing dome that shielded kids and a basketball floor from the weather. Naturally, something this size is beyond the scope of this book. But there is a simple, inexpensive, and fast way of making a play space with poly-film plastic, an electric fan, a roll of wide polytape, and a tube of rolled-up corrugated board. Single-wall is ideal for this construction, although almost any paper product flexible enough to roll and stiff enough to hold its shape will do the trick.

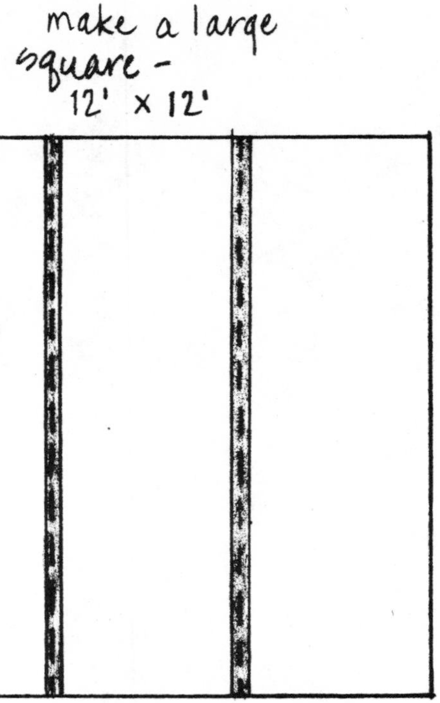

make a large square— 12' x 12'

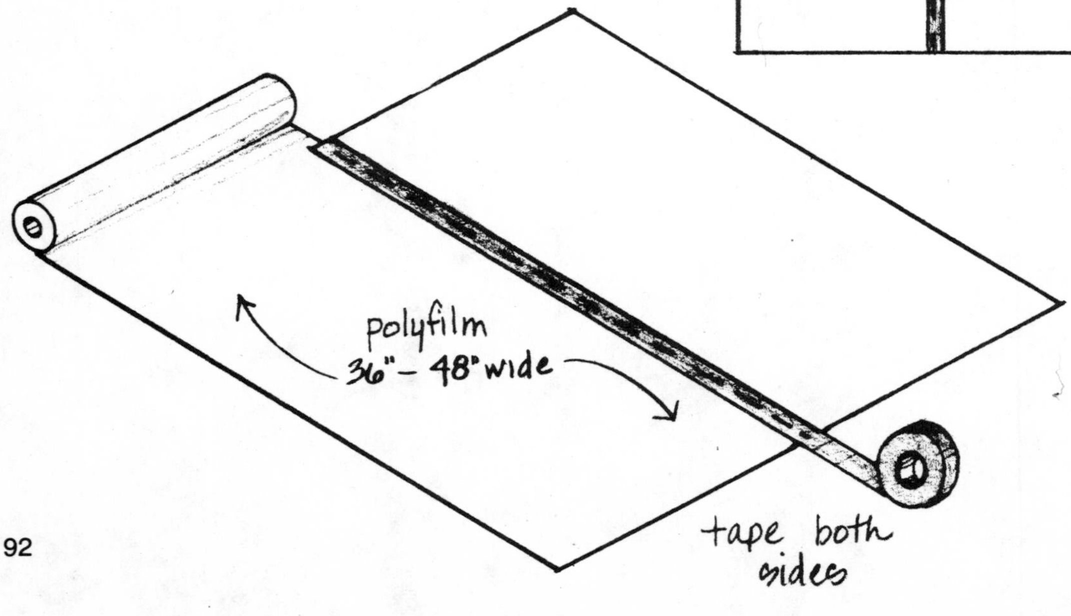

polyfilm 36"– 48" wide

tape both sides

Construction hints. Cut 12' or 15' lengths of polyfilm, place edge to edge, and tape (both sides) to make a big square, as shown. Now fold corners of square toward center and tape on top side. Cut slit near edge for tube.

Roll up corrugated to make tube. It should be big enough to accommodate a small electric fan. Fit tube in slit, plug in fan, and blow cool air into polyfilm bag to inflate.

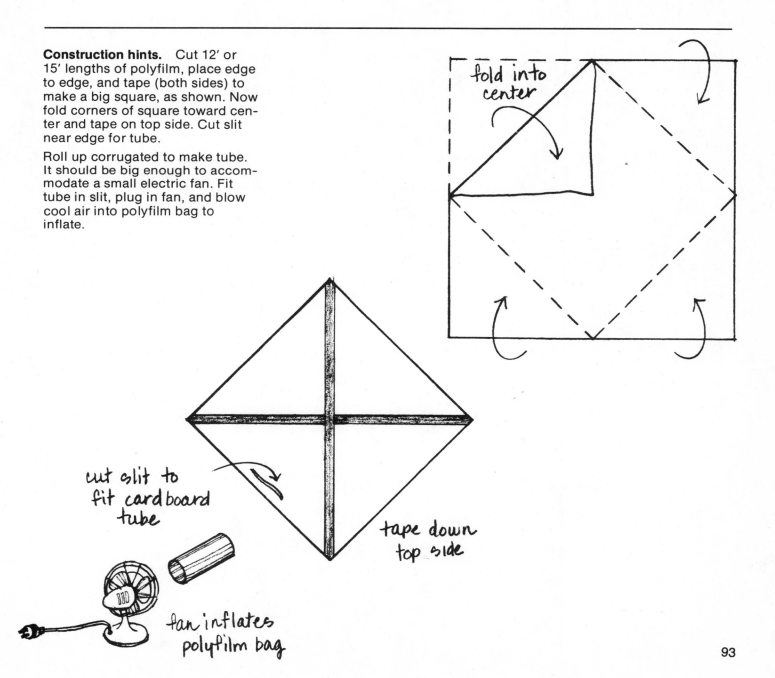

fold into center

cut slit to fit cardboard tube

tape down top side

fan inflates polyfilm bag

Finally, cut another slit low on in-flato-space for crawl-in entry.

As long as the fan is blowing cool air into the polyfilm bag the in-flato-space is a snug, wonderful play space for the kids. Obviously, though, kids will have to take it fairly easy, because the polyfilm skin can rip or puncture. (It is easily repaired with a piece of poly-tape here or there.) Remember, however, you must keep that fan blowing and *you must never leave small children alone in the inflato-space.* Suffocation is always a hazard with plastic structures, and although the danger in this case is not great, don't take any chances. Instead, get inside with them.

You've never felt so much air all around you at once—a bouncing, buoyant feeling!

Once you get a feeling for them, you will need little urging to make larger and larger inflato-spaces. I use "6 mil" polyfilm, which blows up nicely into a room-sized in-flato-space. Remember: it must be big to be fun and really safe.

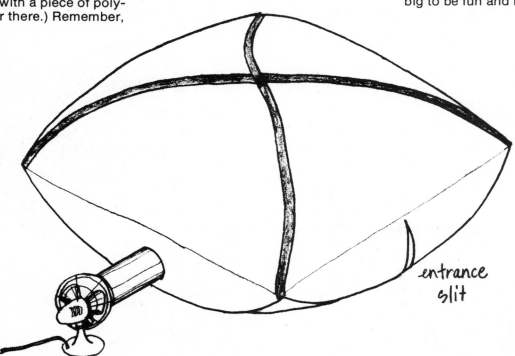

entrance slit

Geoshapes

By now you can cut, score, cement, slot, tab, fold, drill, tape, lace, bolt, saw, slice, and curse much better than before. True? You have either learned to do things you didn't know how to do, learned to do them better, or learned to put your skills to different uses. Now it is time to try some projects that combine some of your new skills and interests while challenging you to be creative as well.

The following design-shapes have been kept abstract. The layouts are such that you can choose your own system of engineering. So, with the kids' help on a rainy weekend, you can do some thinking first and then cut loose.

Incidentally, how many times have I used an expression like "with the kids' help" in this book? Often, because as you know by now, kids can do almost anything you can do, and they expect to work with you. This means you do the pre-figuring and supply the materials, and they'll allow you to help—if you don't try to take over! You may have noticed, too, that their stay-ing power has increased, that they are neater and more manually dexterous. Even the little ones need less help than before. Thus your figuring should run something like this "Which system can they have the most fun using that requires me the least?"

Study each layout and sketch of the assembled structure first, but don't worry about materials or construction yet. How big do you want it to be? Table-top size? A floor model? You will find yourself moving quickly from thoughts about size to ones of function. And from there, the decision on which system to use in building your geoshape should occur naturally.

Cut and fold. Decide whether you want to use single-wall corrugated or true "cardboard" (the noncorrugated variety). Big sheets that will accommodate your entire layout, or several smaller ones? And what kind of cement will you need?

If you're scaling down, for your own sanity do it by easy fractions such as one-half, one-third, or one-fourth. And remember, if you double the size of your working plans (for, say, a floor model), you'll need something large like used appliance cartons.

Lay out your dimensions first, then cut the material, crease, fold, cement, and assemble all at one sitting if possible. Better still, get enough material to make several geoshapes of different sizes, so that people of various ages can work at the same time and in the same room, each at his best speed.

Lace the Geoshape. If your original idea for a geoshape is one scaled to a child aged five, then you probably want to use heavier material—scrap corrugated perhaps—combined with whatever else you can scrounge. In other words, you are going to assemble pieces, not whole sheets, and you need a simple, rapid, child-powered system to do it. Obviously, what you want to make is a laced geoshape.

The process is the same as for making a lacer-space. Figure the sizes, transfer the dimensions, and mark and cut out all the material you're using. Label all pieces A, B, C, D, etc., and use a lacer-jig and drill to punch your holes. Get out the vinyl-sheathed clotheslines and start lacing. Remember to slip a washer in place after you tie the first knot, to prevent pull through. And make sure you have enough washers.

Hub and dowel it. If you decide to use hub and dowels in assembling your geoshape, make certain you have calculated correctly the number of hubs required at intersecting points. Study the sketch well enough so that you don't have to look back at it all the time. (The kids have probably already figured it out!) If you have hubs left over from other projects, this will speed things up. Otherwise, make as many as you will need.

If the sides of the geoshape are not identical, be certain to mark dowels of different length in different colors (e.g., all X-length dowels with a splash of red, all Y-length dowels with a splash of blue). This will prevent mix-ups and frustrations—and also make the assembling process easier.

Before enlarging a hub-and-doweled geoshape, try it according to the dimensions given here first—or make it smaller. Remember, you are teetering on the brink of trigonometry now, and small differences in lengths of dowels are critical. Even with flexible hose hubs, you can't stretch a dowel you've cut 2″ too short. Once you start combining equilateral triangles with isosceles, there's engineering involved, not just cutting, coloring, and joining.

Geoshapes mean learning. Be reassured that no matter how much fun and entertainment lies in making geoshapes, children are learning something, too. They are rapidly mastering space concepts, involving themselves with measurements and math, and playing with concepts in both plane and solid geometry. They are combining what they already know with what they have just discovered. They are experiencing numerous little tremors of recognition and successfully beating back the frustrations that are part of any creative process. They are not only learning as they play and through their play, they are—and this is of the greatest importance—learning how to learn.

If you take time to paint a cardboard prism green and a cubic geoshape red, then rig a blue fabric cover for a hub-and-doweled pyramid, you will be providing learning as well as fun for your kids. They will begin to recognize complicated geometric forms through color—and eventually to call them by their correct names. Kids love long words like "icosahedron" and "duodecahedron"—especially when they know what those words mean because they have actually constructed the shapes that go with them. The unknown has become the familiar and useful, the base for the next plunge into the mysterious. And that is really what learning is all about.

Geoshapes are versatile. One of the most obvious uses for the geoshape made of single-wall or construction paper is as a lamp. The flat panels can be punched or slit for designs on designs rather like old-fashioned tinware lanterns or decoupage shades. The local hardware store or five-and-ten carries all you need in the way of inexpensive sockets, and so forth. The simplest method of on-off switches is a plug, but more aesthetic types can be devised.

Use low-watt bulbs—and I mean low! It is more than likely that you will use your geoshape for decorative purposes, so 25 watts is plenty. Or get hold of some Christmas tree minilights. You can get real bargains on these during the off-season.

Functionality aside, kids like geoshaping because it's easy and it's fun. In less than an hour they can transfer a design, lay it out, cut it out, and assemble it to create a completed structure. They can solve all the problems posed themselves. The completed geoshape demands paint, cutouts, pasting—something else to do. The variety of plane surfaces suggests different coverings—paper, fabric, fake fur, and what-have-you.

Geoshapes are simple space sculptures and intriguing building blocks that seem to invite combining. Kids can glue them together or stack them and cover stacks with fabric to hold them snug. With string and dowels, you can hang them as mobiles. There's as much food for thought in a completed geoshape as there is challenge in its construction.

One small engineer I know, building an innercity complex of octahedrons and prisms, told me in the greatest confidence that they were "look-ats." True—but they're also a lot more besides visual experiences.

Tetrahedron

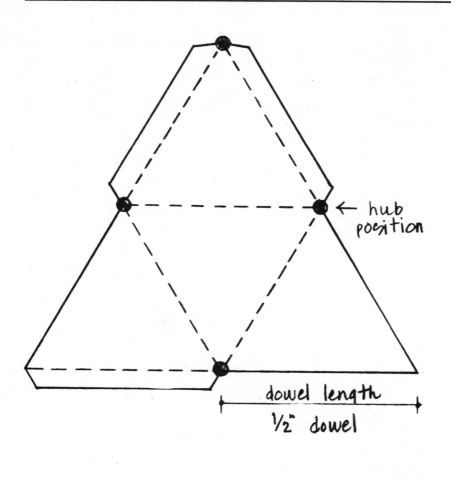

← hub position

dowel length
½" dowel

assembled
tetrahedron

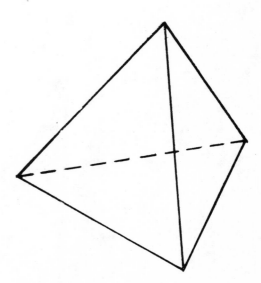

Pyramid with triangle base

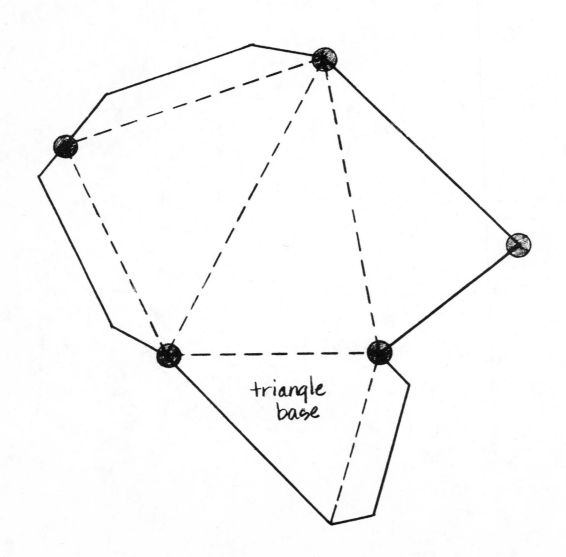

triangle base

Cube

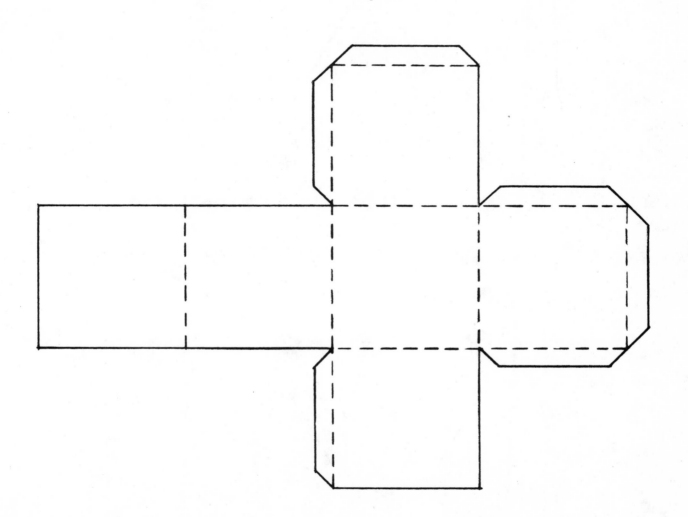

Pyramid with square base

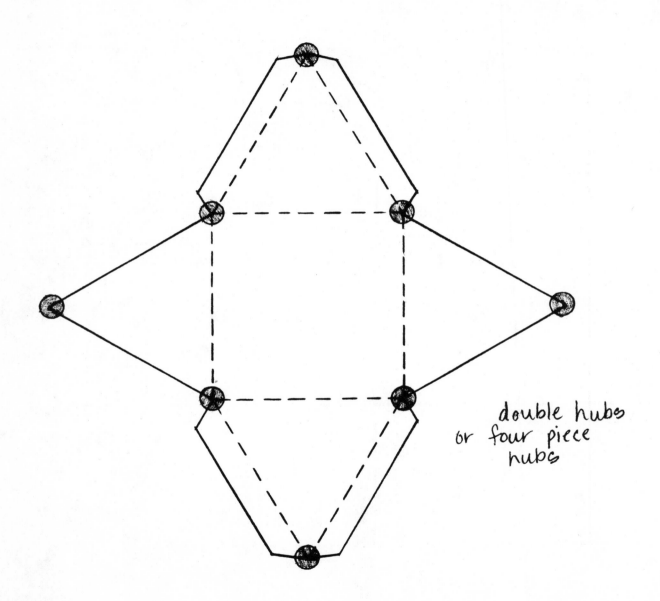

double hubs
or four piece
hubs

Rectangular prism

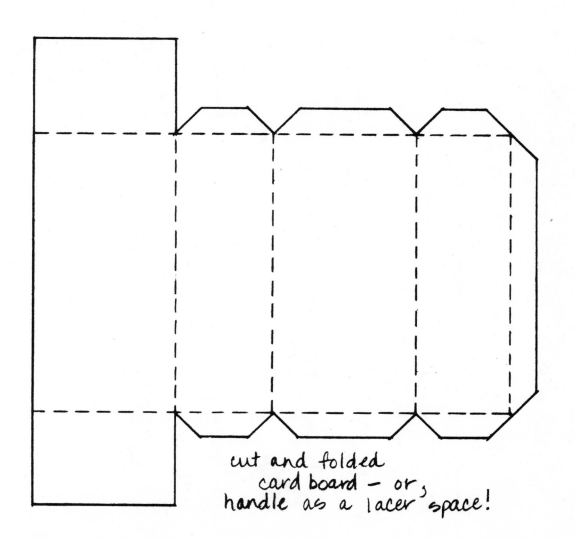

cut and folded
card board — or,
handle as a lacer space!

Triangular prism

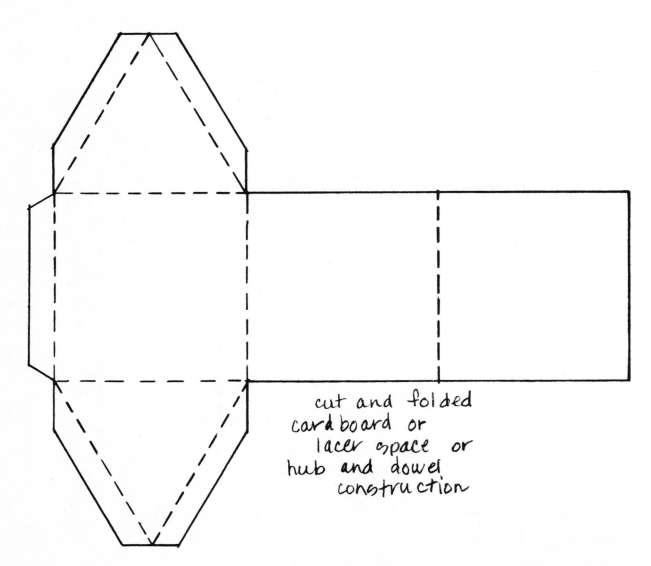

cut and folded
cardboard or
lacer space or
hub and dowel
construction

Prism with square base

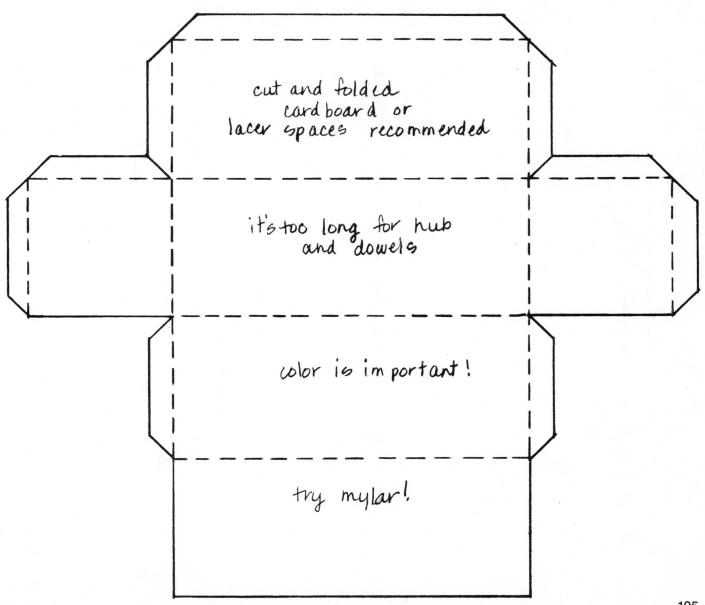

cut and folded
cardboard or
lacer spaces recommended

it's too long for hub
and dowels

color is important!

try mylar!

Hexagonal prism

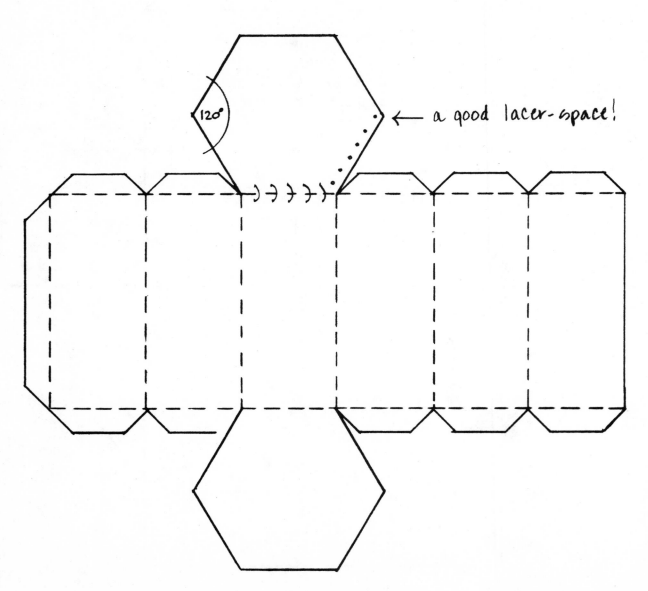

120°

← a good lacer-space!

Octahedron

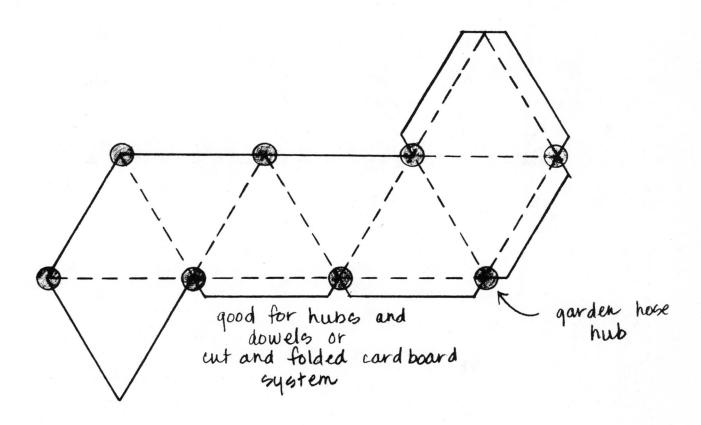

good for hubs and
dowels or
cut and folded cardboard
system

garden hose
hub

Icosahedron

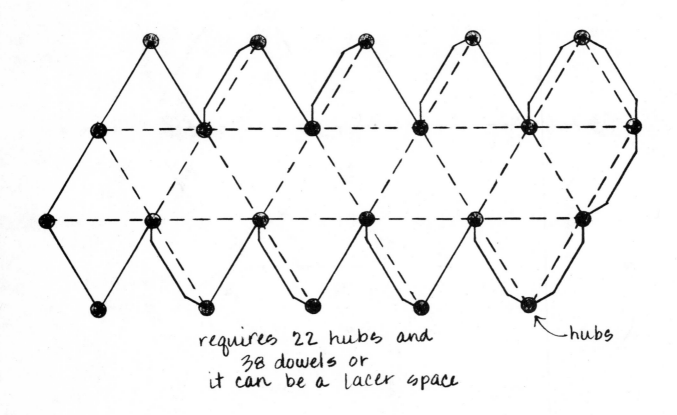

requires 22 hubs and
38 dowels or
it can be a lacer space

hubs

Dodecahedron

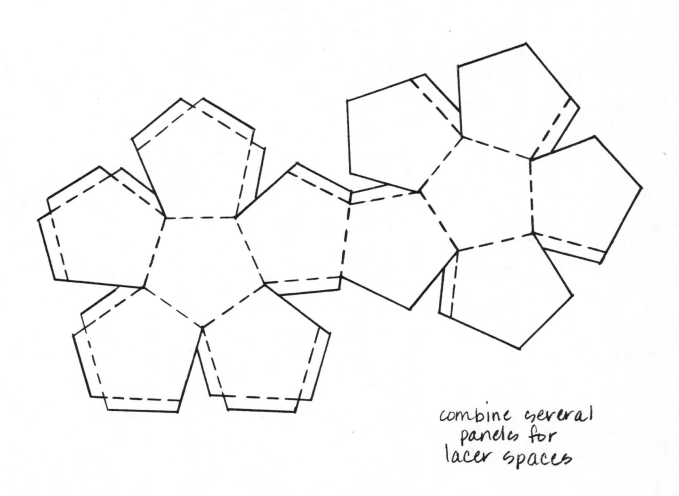

combine several
panels for
lacer spaces

Habitats

The designs on the pages that follow move from the basic to the more elaborate. All the pieces have been designed to knock down for flat storage. The progression is from four flat panels made in multiples that can be expanded into play areas, to four flat panels that slot together to form large but limited play spaces, true rooms, and houses.

Remember that dimensions on the working plans may be scaled down by one-half, one-third, or one-fourth. However, keep in mind that the thickness of triple-wall remains a constant 9/16"— that is, relatively bulky. If you go too small, you'll create problems for yourself.

On the other hand, do not attempt to enlarge these basic designs beyond the sizes given on the working plans unless you are prepared to reinforce the corrugated with wood lathing, plywood strips, and triangular plywood gussets or two-by-fours. Flat sheets of triple-wall have a maximum load-bearing capacity, and if the gap between supports is too great, the sheets will buckle.

As you've noticed, the directions for building have grown less detailed as this book has progressed. The same principle is followed in this section; the more you make, the less you need to be told. There comes a point, certainly, where the interested cardboard craftsman needs only material, work space, and time. Your creativity should take over where mine begins to falter.

Many adults enjoy work as a process, but kids generally like to jump from the idea to the accomplished object as soon as possible. Thus, whatever is built should be made available to them for play *at once*. You can always paint it later, when they're napping or at school or when they finally express some desire for colors and textures on their construction. And resist the urge for neatness and elegance. Don't impose your values on them— they're still children.

These habitats may be used outside and around, next to, or with any of the cardboard furniture designs included in the first part of this book. As you will see, kids have a way of making almost anything into a "house."

Habitat I

Habitat 1 is the simplest, most flexible play space of its type—and perhaps the best one for your kids. It is excellent for small, active children, and its panels can be built, taken apart, and re-formed in an almost infinite variety of creative spaces and shapes for use indoors or out, at home or in school.

Construction hints. Cut and slot panels according to size from material you like and think your kids will work best with. Be lavish and inventive with foam, fabric, or reflecting plastics like Mylar. Panels can be walls, ceiling, bulletin boards, color-ons, or tack boards. Triple-wall is strong enough to take many hours of hard use, and it is much less expensive than tempered masonite. When working with triple-wall, cut the slots at least ⅝" wide and tape them to minimize wear and tear. Masonite, a more rigid and heavier material, will require snugger slots (5/16")

The panels indicated on the diagram may, of course, be altered according to your wishes and needs. Why not scale down all dimensions by one-half or one-third? The sizes chosen for these designs make for quick reductions in scale. But unless you have a great deal of play space in a desert climate, don't go any bigger. Triple-wall and masonite are subject to warping, and both lose strength if the gaps between structural members are too wide.

Incorporate fake furs and shaggy carpet remnants, wallpaper, Contac paper, and irridescent paints into your design. Remember also to provide old sheets, cheap plastic dropcloths, or wide sheets of polyfilm for additional play ideas that the kids will be quick to invent.

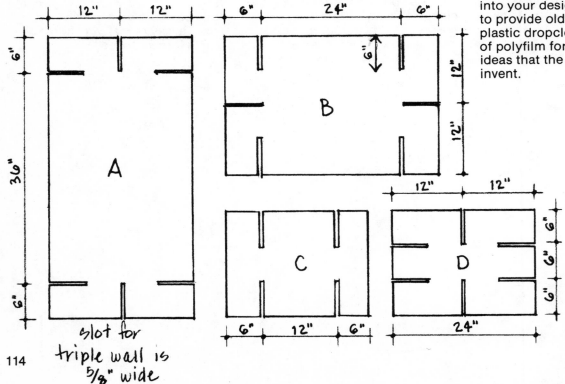

slot for triple wall is ⅝" wide

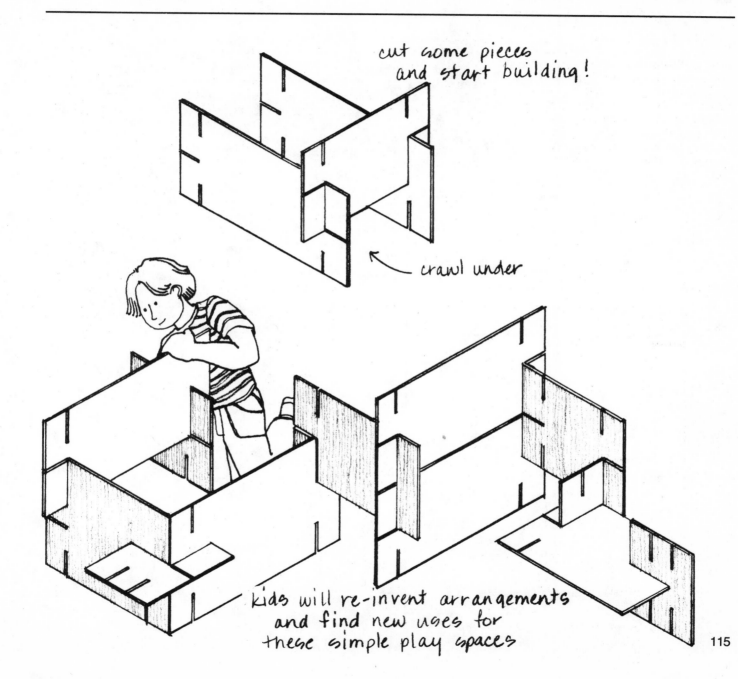

cut some pieces
and start building!

← crawl under

kids will re-invent arrangements
and find new uses for
these simple play spaces

Store/theater

Materials

scrap corrugated

triple-wall corrugated, 4′ × 6′

tape

acrylic enamel and brush

mat knife

ruler or other straightedge

marking pen or pencil

Another very simple structure, this can be decorated according to use. But don't be surprised if the kids prefer to tape and paint it themselves. And do not attempt to make this a permanent structure. As long as it can be changed it is somehow alive and better, especially for younger children whose imaginations are always so active.

Measure and mark according to layout. Cut out pieces from 4′ × 6′ corrugated and slot together. Use scrap corrugated to make a ticket booth, a dressing room for puppets or players, or a storage room for make-believe merchandise.

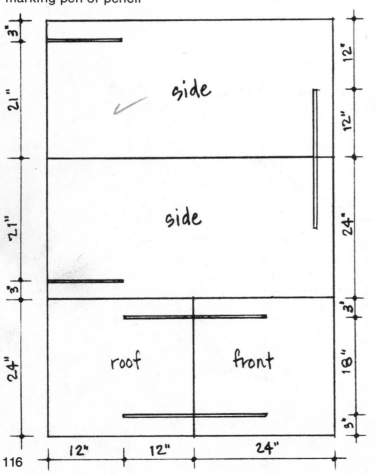

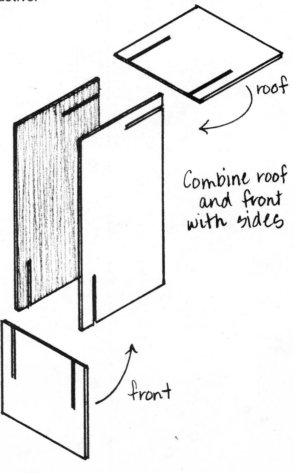

roof

Combine roof and front with sides

front

116

for a
puppet show or
a make-believe
store!

Dice house

Materials

four pieces triple-wall, 4' × 6'
scrap triple-wall

tape

acrylic enamel and brush

mat knife

string

marking pen or pencil

ruler or other straightedge

bolts, washers, wing-nuts for
braces (optional)

This triple-wall cube construction
is very popular with younger
children. It can be played in, on,
and around. Although normally it
is painted white outside and black
inside to create the illusion of a
giant die, the panels can be re-
versed. Or why not paint them in
other contrasting colors such as
red and green, blue and yellow,
or whatever?

Since the portholes encourage
climbing, consider the safety of
assembling the dice house on
newspaper padding or foam for
indoor play, or setting it up in sand
or sawdust outdoors. The size of
panels prevents tipping over.
Several gymnasts can cling to and
scramble up any side and the
structure will stay put.

Construction hints. As diagram
shows, each panel is a square, 48"
× 48", cut from 4' × 6' triple-wall
sheets. The slots, as usual, are just
over one-half the height of panels
—about 24".

Calculating the position of the
portholes is easy. All you need is
string, a pencil, and a yardstick.
Find the center of panel 1 by run-
ning two lengths of string diago-
nally from the corners. Where they
cross, X marks the spot that will be
the center of the largest porthole.
Kids can use this one as a door.
Mark the circle and cut it free.

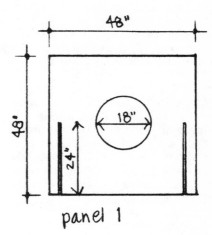

panel 1

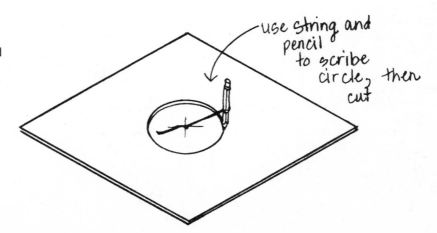

use string and
pencil
to scribe
circle, then
cut

Position the portholes on panel 2 for "snake-eyes," with a single length of string stretched corner to corner as shown. Now dazzle the kids by applying the Pythagorean Theorum. The string is the hypotenuse of a right triangle, and its square is equal to the sum of the squares of the other two sides. Compute the sum of (48 × 48) + (48 × 48), then simply take the square root (approximately 68) and divide it by 3. Measure this distance (22 2/3″) along the string, beginning at the lower corner, and mark it. Or do it a simpler way—visually, with two bits of colored paper. Place one piece about one-third of the way up the string, the other about one-third of the way down. Now measure with the ruler and readjust until paper markers are approximately equidistant. Mark. Using these points as the centers, cut out two circles. Follow the dimensions indicated on layout.

Panel 3 is worked in the same way, but using three pieces of colored paper to mark off distances. When papers appear equidistant, mark the spots and cut. Precision is not required; this is a play space for children. Obviously, the three portholes on panel 3 will be smaller than the two on panel 2, which will in turn be smaller than the one on panel 1. You weaken the structure if you cut too many large holes in a given panel, so again, follow the dimensions shown.

Panel 4 has four portholes. Lay out a square within the square shape of the panel itself. Follow dimensions given in layout. Now cut out circles.

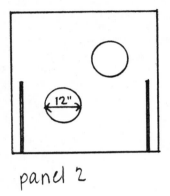

panel 2

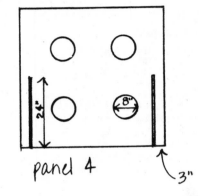

panel 4

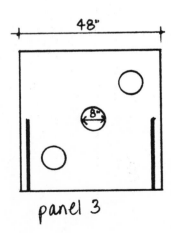

panel 3

Since panels will warp and slots are deep, brace pieces of triple-wall are a good idea. These should be taped first, then glued into position on the *outside* of panel before any panel is painted. (Contact cement bonds triple-wall beautifully to triple-wall, but not to paint.) Braces can also be bolted into position.

Tape portholes next, using short pieces of 1″ or 1½″ masking tape, overlapped. Press each strip firmly against cut edge, then slit the overlap into flaps no longer than 2″ with a mat knife, razor blade (single edge), or X-acto knife. Press each flap down on panel, inside and out. Don't skimp with materials here. These port-holes are doors and windows, hand holds and foot rests; they get a lot of hard use.

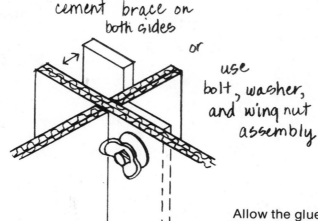

cement brace on both sides

or use bolt, washer, and wing nut assembly

Allow the glued braces to dry overnight. Check the taped portholes and smooth down any flaps you have missed. You will need help in assembling the play space because panels are bulky and heavy, and they take some careful maneuvering. Don't break off the flaps when you slide panels together. The slots must be wide enough to accommodate corrugated as it is slipped in, but the fit should be snug. The braces will provide added strength that may surprise you. This is a rugged object you have created.

Now climb inside the dice house and paint the interior walls. If you're too big and it's too small, have the kids do it. Paint the exterior with two, even three coats, especially where portholes are taped. This way you will be certain panels will not warp. The result is a true cube shape, aesthetically pleasing to adults and a delight for children to play in.

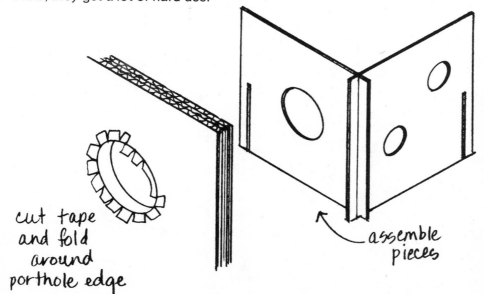

cut tape and fold around porthole edge

assemble pieces

Angle house

Materials

four sheets triple-wall corrugated, 4' × 6'

four ¾" dowels, 4" long

contact cement

tape

mat knife

ruler or other straightedge

triple-wall for scrap braces, bolts, washers, wing-nuts (optional)

acrylic enamel and brush

This large play space requires only four panels and some scrap braces. Two sides are identical. One roof panel slips into slots, the other takes two tabs and four dowels. For small children, you can reduce your dimensions by half or one-quarter, and you can also use double-wall instead of triple-wall.

If you use plywood the structure will be particularly strong, but it will also be quite heavy and expensive to build.

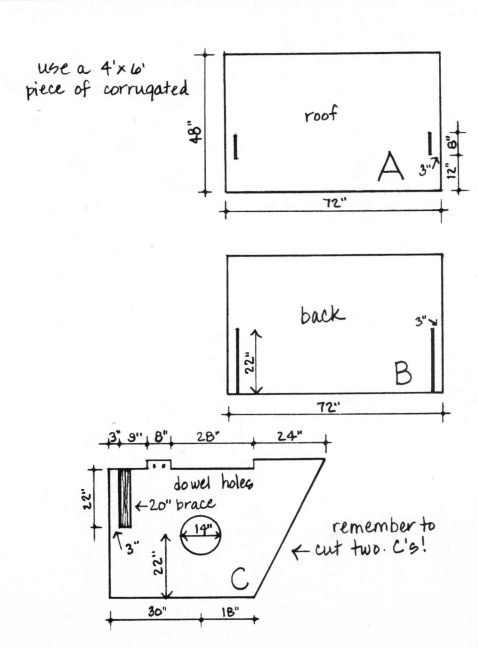

Construction hints. Make your roof panels first. Assistant architects can tape and paint these (on both sides to minimize warp) while you measure and mark other pieces.

The tabs are long and will break off unless you make braces (see layout). However, the depth of slots does give angle house greater strength.

Sand the rough edges of your dowels. Do not cut holes for the dowels in side panels until house is partially assembled. Instead, cut out portholes.

With details taken care of, you are 90 percent done already. Gather together your construction crew. One child can hold a side panel (C_1) in place while you slide roof panel B into its slot. Easy does it. Now hold B and C up in the air and slide the other side (C_2) into its slot. The three pieces will stand up while roof panel A is dropped over the tabs.

Now put the butt of a dowel against the tab and draw around it. Make only two holes on each tab. Mark on both sides. Disassemble the structure and cut dowel holes. This way you will get a nice snug fit.

Tape and glue braces, or bolt into position on the *inside* of panel. Tape portholes carefully, as before. Allow braces to dry. Now reassemble angle house, slipping dowels in position over roof panels.

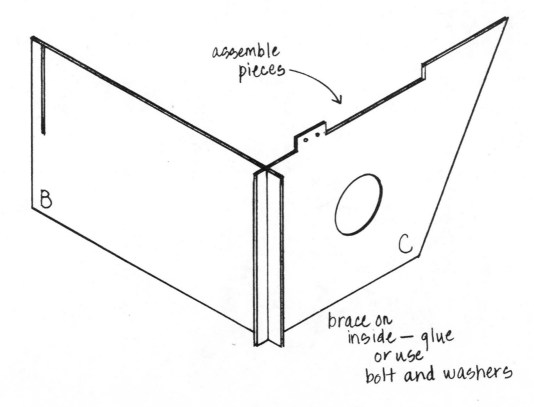

assemble pieces

B

C

brace on inside — glue or use bolt and washers

The angle house can be used as a garage for tricycles, a ship, a store, a cave, or just a plain playhouse.

The broad flat surfaces may worry some mothers. Will kids break the triple-wall if they climb on it? It may bend eventually, if kids are really rough, but it will never break.

The large-size angle house is too big for inside set-ups in most homes or apartments. (That idea may not appeal to kids anyway; it is a house and therefore needs land.) So, out into the yard with it —or to a park. Properly finished with acrylic enamel, angle house can be left out overnight in heavy rain without damage. When the kids get bored, take it down for storage. Or you could bolt the side panels to two-by-fours as the frame for a tent (for two), easily transported in a station wagon or VW bus. Rig drop netting to screen out the bugs.

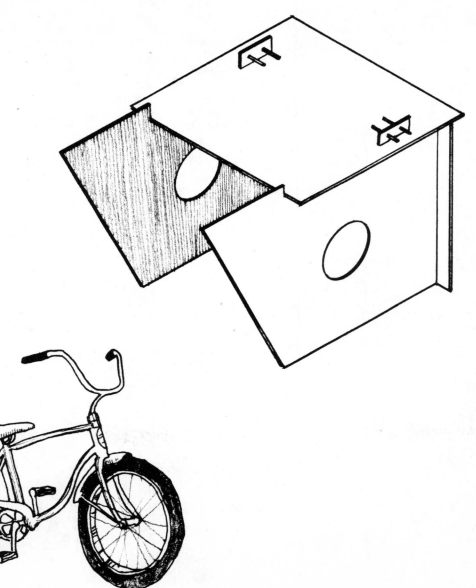

Trucks and other vehicles

Almost before a basic design is completed, kids usually give me suggestions on how to improve or alter a shape or assembly system. An idea or shape may freeze in an adult's mind, but children tend to be less rigid in their thinking. While the average small child cannot render three-dimensional objects in a drawing or painting, he will naturally and easily build them if he has the materials.

Given the basic box of side panels and brace panels described here, you can do the school bus and then go on to any truck shapes your engineering staff can dream up. Obviously, you can enclose the top by adding another panel cut 43⅞" × 72". Now, omit the windows and you have a moving van, suitable for a bright, splashy paint job.

Or why not a cab? A pint-sized pick-up truck? A Volkswagen bus? Different paint, some blankets tossed into the back, perhaps a cloth-and-dowel tent rigged off the rear, and everybody is camping out.

Perhaps you are an elementary school teacher, or you know someone who is. Combine construction with another learning objective: map-reading skills. Where are the national parks in your state and what's at each one? The kids can "ride" in their bus or camper, figuring the mileage and doing simple time, rate, and distance problems. This will get them prepared for slides or a film on any place they choose to "go."

A nail, a broomstick, another corrugated disk, and some tape will make a dandy steering wheel for the school bus driver. Expect to observe some interesting games such as "Smash-up," "Pollution," and even (quite recently) "Hijack." These merry activities suggest to me that while the school bus may be the most familiar form of transportation for kids, it's not necessarily their favorite.

School bus

Materials

three pieces triple-wall, 48″ × 72″

four ⅛″ dowels, 3″ long

four wide rubberbands

masking tape

yellow acrylic enamel, black acrylic enamel, and paint brush

mat knife

marking pen or pencil

ruler or other straightedge

Step 1:
Lay out right and left sides on triple-wall sheets, marking windows and slots with pen. Cut out sides, allowing ⅜″ extra relief for slot depth. On left side only, mark and cut out door.

Step 2:
Now lay out four brace panels on third piece of triple-wall. Mark and cut. Slot all brace panels.

Step 3:
Cut out two wheels from scrap door panel. Cut other two wheels from additional scrap.

Tape all rough edges on door, windows, and wheels. Assemble bus body as shown. Paint bright yellow (two coats) and letter top-front and top-back brace panels.

Paint wheels on both sides. Position over projecting flaps of lower brace panels. Push in sharpened dowels for wheel axles. Now twist rubberbands over dowels to hold wheels in place.

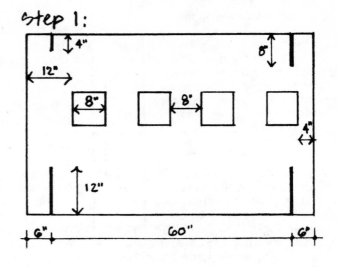

step 1:

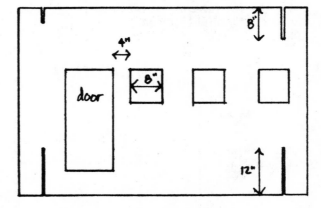

step 3:

door cut out

additional scrap

128

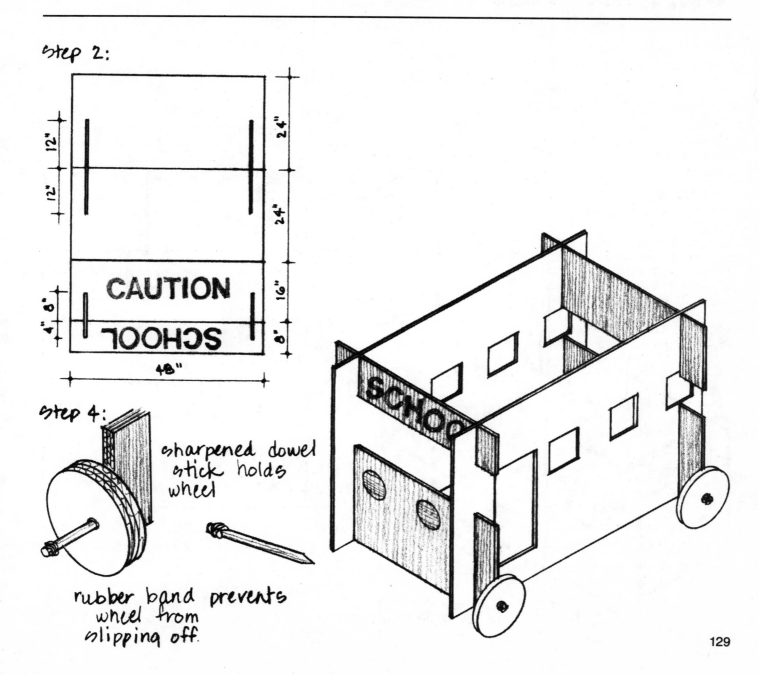

step 2:

12"
12"
24"
24"
16"
8"
8"
4"
48"

CAUTION
SCHOOL

step 4:

sharpened dowel
stick holds
wheel

rubber band prevents
wheel from
slipping off.

SCHOO

129

Vehicle variations

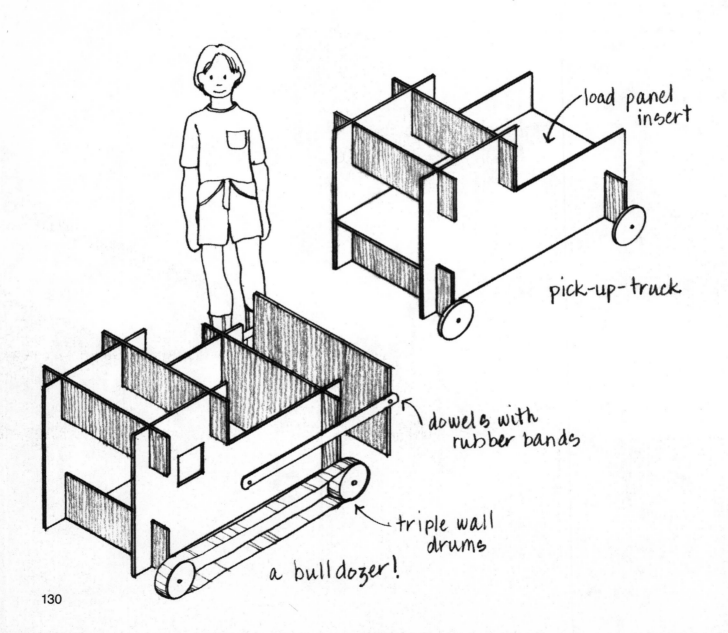

load panel insert

pick-up-truck

dowels with rubber bands

triple wall drums

a bulldozer!

Bunny starters

I remember a professor when I was in graduate school who liked to stir sluggish minds by starting off his classes with some outrageous remark, either borrowed or invented. His words would invariably cause heads to snap up, jaws to drop, and the seminar would begin with a bang. By way of explanation, he confided to us one day that if you tossed a few rocks into a field of long grass, rabbits hidden there would bound away. Hence, the name for this chapter: "Bunny-Starters."

The sketches that follow are to start you thinking and making some school vacation-sized projects. To complete such a project you will need to apply all the Scavenger's Rules, plus your own design and building skills. You may even need another adult to help—and certainly all the kids. The drawings, again, are rough approximations, *not plans,* and no dimensions are given. Size will depend on the amount of time you have, the materials you're using, and the ages of the kids.

Perhaps because I also write novels, I tend to think in terms of large, complex structures. And perhaps because I live on a farm and am usually busy working, I think that work itself is fun. But kids like big things, too, provided the parts can be played with as they go along. What bores them is a big thing that is a "no-no" until it is finished. (And "finished" is really a relative term, anyway.) Any single step completed is obviously a thing done. The ship-in-the-building, for instance, is any number of things—a tent, a house, a store.

Build not according to plan but according to what you have. Expect and look for change as you go. The kids will toss a few stones into your field, so be prepared to do some jumping.

A final note: the bigger the project, the more costly it will be. Scavenge for everything. And how will you store your bunny-starter when it is not in use? Maybe it is going to be a church-school project, a do-it-together-with-the-neighbors, or a play-group activity. Think of people, not of plans, the possible, not the unlikely. If play is truly the work that children do, then let your work become play.

A me-tree

In elementary school, kids often make likenesses of themselves on large pieces of paper and then color in their features and clothing. The same idea executed in double- or triple-wall corrugated and set on a base becomes a piece of human sculpture that can be used to hang clothes on. Call it a "me-tree" and hope it will encourage kids to be a little neater!

Have your child lie flat on a large piece of corrugated. Draw around him and cut out figure. Then have him lie sideways. Draw around again and cut out.

Cut side view in half horizontally. Remember the slot rule: a slot equals one-half the total height of panel. Cut slots in side view, then flat view. Slide views together, provide paints, brushes, and cast-off clothing, and spread some papers out. What does a child look like to himself? Yarn or excelsior hair? Button eyes, glued on? A worn-out but still favorite shirt stapled to the torso. What are his hands holding? A lamp? Try a photographer's spring clamp.

A me-tree will tip unless you put a toy soldier base on the bottom of the basic X-brace. Allow plenty of material, at least 24" each way.

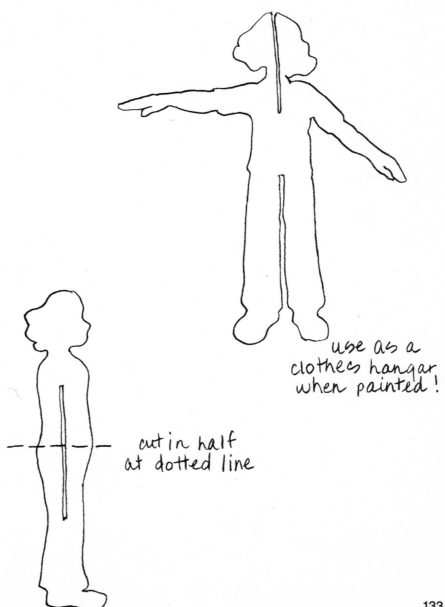

use as a clothes hanger when painted!

cut in half at dotted line

133

Racing car

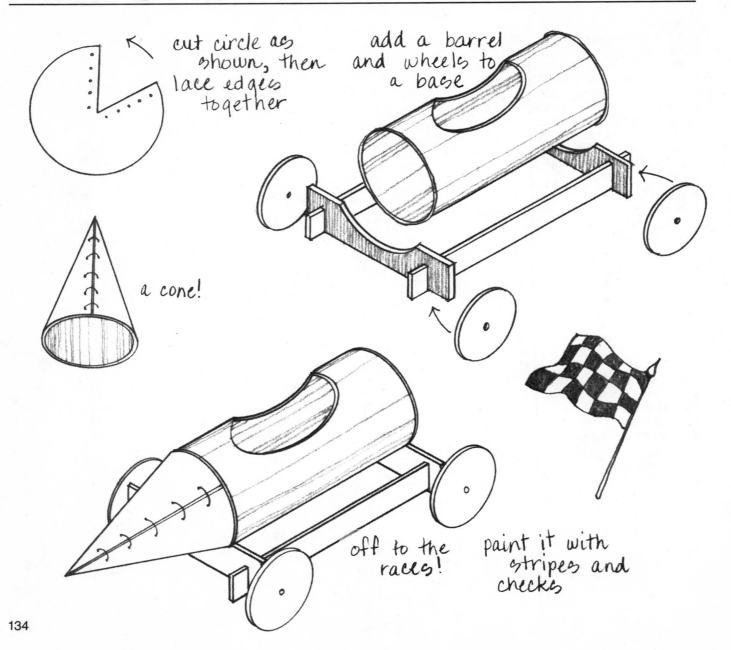

cut circle as shown, then lace edges together

add a barrel and wheels to a base

a cone!

off to the races!

paint it with stripes and checks

Indoor aircraft

A bunny box

You can design and build a kid-sized bunny-box for use in a room or outside. Use corrugated panels (with cutouts) and blackboard paint. Start it small, but make it strong: it should be reinforced with lumber. (Cross-braces and struts are not shown in the diagram, but they are definitely needed.) Add an old ladder. Old nets. Swings and slides. A fireman's pole. A front door from me-tree scrap. Canvas-drop walls. Whatever you have. Whatever you want.

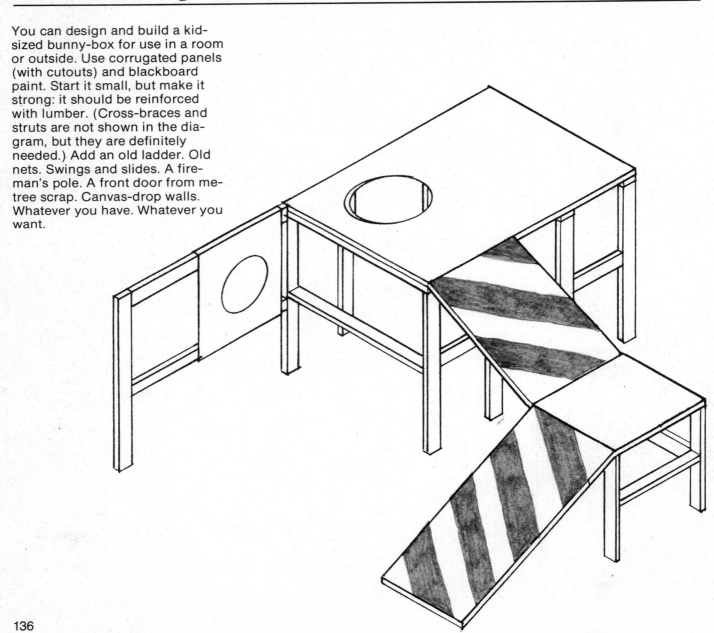

Appendix

Triple-wall suppliers

Triple-wall corrugated is not as readily available as we would like it to be. Hopefully in the near future it will be more so. In the meantime, Tri-Wall Containers, Inc. is one source where triple-wall corrugated can be obtained.

Tri-Wall Containers supplies triple-wall corrugated primarily to educational organizations, to school workshops, etc. Their minimum order is rather steep for one individual. If you are embarking on triple-wall projects, it would be well to involve a few other people to split the cost and the order. Community play groups and day care centers should not, however, have this problem.

Triple-wall is available from Tri-Wall in four sizes.—42" x 54", 4' x 5', 4' x 6', 4' x 8'. Except for the 42" x 54" size, which is available in a minimum lot of twenty sheets, the minimum order is 100 boards.

Orders for Tri-Wall can be placed with any of the following three branches.

Tri-Wall Containers, Inc.
100 Crossways Park West
Woodbury, New York, 11797
Tel: (516) 364-2800

Tri-Wall Containers, Inc.
Butler, Indiana 46721
Tel: (219) 868-2151

Tri-Wall Containers, Inc.
7447 No. Blackstone Avenue
Pinedale, California 93659
Tel: (209) 439-5222

Size	20-99 boards	100 boards
42" x 54"	$3.66 per board	$2.05 per board
4' x 5'	unavailable	$2.60 per board
4' x 6'	unavailable	$3.15 per board
4' x 8'	unavailable	$4.39 per board

Tools to use with cardboard

The Workshop For Learning Things, Inc. designed special tools to use only with cardboard, including Tri-wall corrugated. Although you can use the basic tools and equipment mentioned in this book successfully, you should know that the following are available, separately or as part of an Accessory Tool Kit, from Workshop For Learning Things, Inc., 5 Bridge Street, Watertown, Massachusetts 02172.

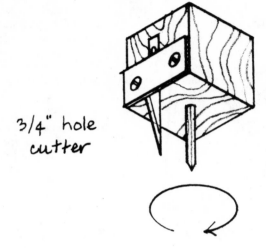

3/4" hole cutter

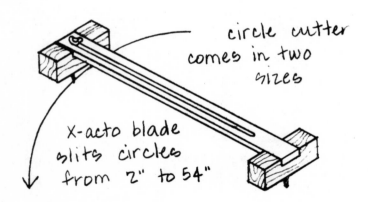

circle cutter comes in two sizes

X-acto blade slits circles from 2" to 54"

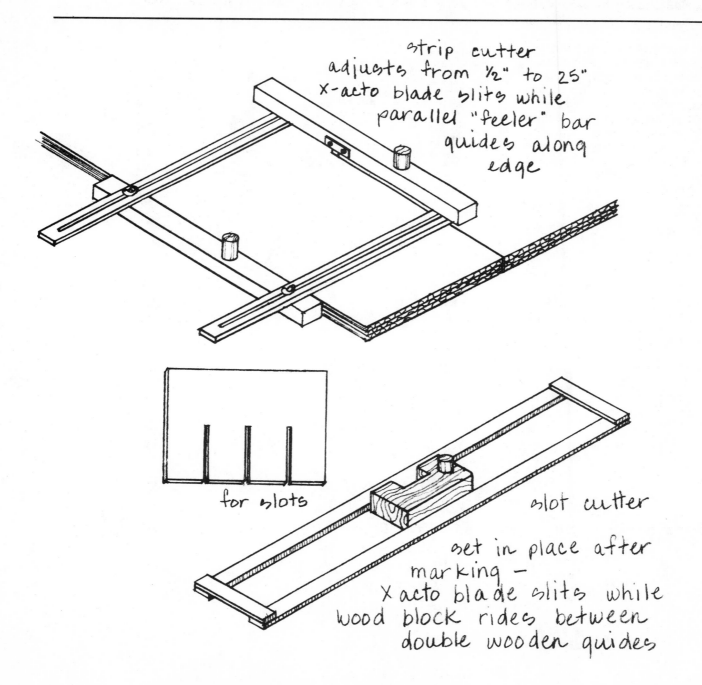

strip cutter
adjusts from ½" to 25"
x-acto blade slits while
parallel "feeler" bar
guides along
edge

for slots

slot cutter

set in place after
marking —
X-acto blade slits while
wood block rides between
double wooden guides

141

Coupling systems

Ordinary hardware fasteners are not always satisfactory for cardboard construction. To join pieces of cardboard or to add strength to your structures use these coupling systems which are obtainable at hardware stores and lumber yards.

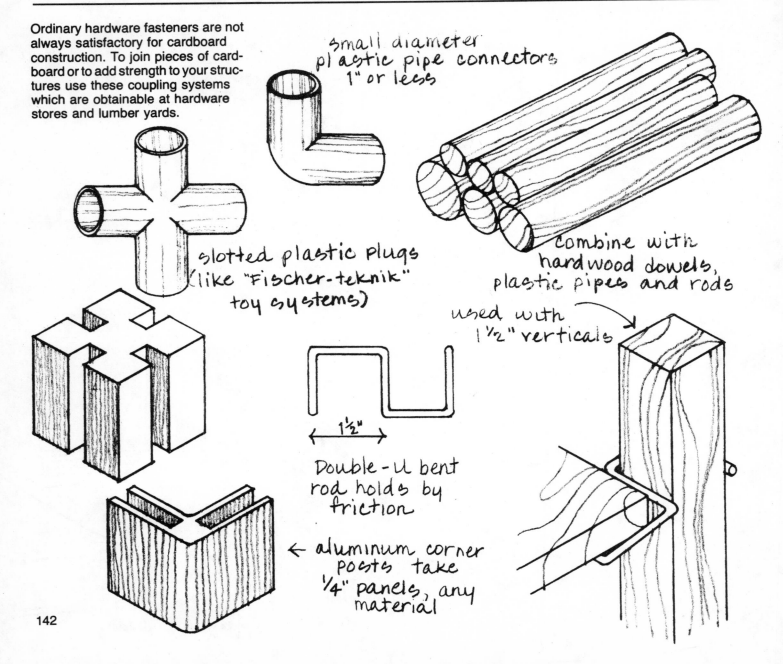

small diameter plastic pipe connectors 1" or less

slotted plastic plugs (like "Fischer-teknik" toy systems)

combine with hardwood dowels, plastic pipes and rods

used with 1½" verticals

1½"

Double-U bent rod holds by friction

← aluminum corner posts take ¼" panels, any material

Notes

Notes